I0441377

Douglas Dauntless Speaks out for Freedom

Mr. Douglas Dauntless

ISBN: 1-4486-9266-0
ISBN-13: 9781448692668

Preface: I would like to acknowledge Robert Chandler's book Shadow World. This book opened my eyes and I understood what is really going on in the United States and the World.

I used this book as a reference to some of my articles, from there I went on the Internet to educate my self and understand more, from there I formed my own opinions which I believe to be true, and I am right.

Douglas Dauntless

Obama taught what...?

While watching the Main-Stream News Media, CNN, a female news caster, I thought she was going to faint when she when she defended Obama and told the every one watching CNN, that "Barrack Hussein Obama was a law professor and taught Constitutional Law. I almost fell out of my chair. Obama was a lecturer at the Chicago University, an extreme leafiest school, who brain wash the young students who have no life experience at all to hate America that America is the worst Country in the World and so on and so on. Obama taught Law students Saul Alinsky "Rules for Radicals" but never taught Constitutional Law, I doubt very much if he ever read it and if he did I don't think he understood it. what Obama does understand are two things; how to be a street organizer and how to use Antonio Gramsci new Communist Manifesto who to use and how to use them. Use the poor and promise them that they will be given free housing, free land free everything, and tell the working guy who thinks that the rich are against him that he, Obama as President will tax the rich to death so that they can live in the Democratic and Republican Marxist Utopia which is another lie. If you want to see a real Marxist Utopia take a good look at Cuba.

Before Castro took over Cuba, with the help of the USA, giving him money and arms and telling us he, Castro wanted a Democracy, and he told the Cuban people he was going to free them, and redistribute the land, take from the rich and give to the poor. The first thing he did was form a strong alliance with Communist Russia, the next thing he did was throw out every American that had a business there other then the gambling casinos which he threw them out also. Now Castro, like Robin Hood of Old took every think from the rich and everything from the poor and kept it all. Just like our Marxist Democrats always saying they want to make everyone equal, Castro did that, he made every one equal, every one was poor. The only rich people in Cuba are Castro and his top aids. That is Obama's plan for America.

Obama never taught law at the Chicago U., he taught Radicalism, how to steal votes with an organization like ACORN in back of him. If Obama taught law a C.U. for twelve years when did he have time to teach anything, if he was organizing on the street, and shooting hoops all day with the gangs and being a Illinois State Senator for seven years and never wrote a law but some else did and handed it to him to read on the Senate floor. Every one that work for Obama, Axelrod, and the Obama Clinton Cabinet along with the Main-News Media are pouring out propaganda that he was a Law Professor, he wrote books, when did he have time, they embellish his life to the public who they think are stupid and believe everything they say about Obama. Well the people have news for every one they don't believe the Main-Stream News Media. Obama is a puppet who strings are being pulled by the super Rich and is given money hand over fist to help Bankrupt the United States along with the Marxist Democrats and Re-publicans who reach across the isle to help each other get rich by destroying our Country. You want to know whose fault it is why we are on the brink of destruction…IT IS OUR FALT FOR NOT PAYING AT-TENTION TO WHO WE VOTED FOR. Every one vot-ed Democrat party line. 90% of the people don't know what Democracy is. It is not what they think it is or were told what it is. We were a Republic be-fore The Elitist Wilson and his man Col. House took over and changed us into a Democracy, where the active minority rules the inactive majority. US.

WAKE UP AMERICA we are in the fight of our lives right now. Join the Tea Party on July4th and march on Washington in September! We have to show this ruling minority that we mean business, they work for us we don't work for them.

A great example of misinformation and propaganda

I read an article on the internet from Reuters, the title, "Obama wins praise at the summit, at the meeting in Port of Spain. What is Obama trying to tell the American public that he told Castro and the other 33 Latin American counties that he would like to see more "Democracy" in Cuba and the Latin American Countries? Who does he think that he is kidding, not the United States where he is forcing Marxism on the United States of America! Does he and his propaganda machine, David Axelrod, brought up by Liberal parents, Liberal at the time was the new word for Communist, his mother Myril who was a writer for a Radical Leftist magazine called PM, a Communist publication, and Rohm Emanuel a Communist head of the Obama administration?

Why are all the Latin American Countries happy to talk to Obama because he is a Marxist just like Castro, Chavez, and Da Silva, they are called the Big Three of Latin America who are changing Latin America into one big Marxist Nation who along with China, Iran, and Russia have all promised to bring the United States of America to it's knees. Knowing how Obama thinks and lies along with the House traitor Nancy Pelosi, Reid, Boxer, and Feinstein, and all the Marxist Democrats and Republicans Obama is selling out the United States of America to Castro, Chavez and da Silva right now. Obama nor the 2006 Marxist Democrats and Republicans who call themselves Liberal really means Communists will give to the Big Three Marxist Latin American Countries any thing they want as long as they will let Obama believe he will run the show and take over everything from the tip of South America to Alaska. I would have liked to have heard what Obama promised the Big Three behind closed doors. To be sure close the Marine Corps Base at Guantanamo Bay that has been a knife in Castro's side for over fifty years. To Brazil he will probably give them the secrets to build an atomic plant that will make low enriched uranium to sell to all the terrorists Countries who are against America, right now it looks like over half of the Countries in the World that are changing to Marxism and Islam are against us and with the help of Obama they just might do that.

Chavez with all his oil money and he gets billions from America with his gas stations through out the United States is the money behind the Big Three of Latin America converting Latin America to Marxism so where is Obama going he is a confirmed Marxist. Obama has no love for America or the people, number one hate the middle class who he will destroy, he is using the "poor" as an excuse to turn America to Marxism.

What kind of a sellout did he give Chavez? How much money will Chavez give him to help the Big Three into turning every thing into a Marxist State under one leadership Obama? Or will the Big Three after using Obama and the Marxist Democrats and Republicans destroy all these people because there will be no room for any one who belongs to the most hated of all the Latin American Countries, the United States of America.

Obama thinks he is the greatest thing that lives on this earth, because and only because of his Marxist thinking and Soros putting into his mind that he will be god like and rule the World. As always a Radical Organizer he has found the one thing in common in Latin America and that is they hate America and Obama will try and use his organizing skills to meld them to him, he thinks that he can talk any one into his thinking. The Big Three are all ringing their hands they have finally found some one who thinks he is to smart for the World and they can out smart and out think Obama in a blink of an eye. Obama is told what to do, he has no control over anything he is just a empty suit who can't speak a word with out an ear phone or teleprompters telling him what to say and do. With out the third Clinton administration in place doing all his thinking for him he hasn't got the brains for the Presidency. Wake up America Obama is now selling us out to Castro, Chavez, Da Silva the Big Three Marxist Countries of Latin America.

Cold blooded killers
By Douglas
Dauntless

Nancy Pelosi went to see the Pope a few weeks ago and after her audience with the Pope told the news media that she and he had a good conversation about this and that and that they agreed about Global Warming. Not exactly true, the Pope told her if she was Catholic and she helped push thru Obama's law to murder babies who survived an abortion, that the Doctor was obligated by law to murder that child, she is not a Catholic.

Nancy Pelosi is not a true Catholic nor is she a kind hearted women, nor does she think that she has done anything wrong by voting to murder babies born alive after a botched abortion. What is the difference between her and Hitler murdering innocent men, women and children, and anyone else that the Nazis wanted to medically experiment with these people while they were still alive doesn't she or Obama realize how many thousand of children she and Obama have condemned to death. Then there are the Doctors who are willing to comment murder because the New Socialist Democrats with the lead of Obama and Nancy Pelosi have voted to kill these poor babies in cold blood. If Nancy Pelosi can go to sleep at night with a clear conscience she is nothing more than a stone, cold blooded killer.

In our Constitution it says that everyone has a right to live, that includes partial birth babies where is the law of man to protect these unfortunate children, where is any law maker in the United States to say this is murder and it is wrong. Every body weather people realizes it or not have a God given right to live. Nancy Pelosi is a mother where is her compassion for these children that she has helped be condemned to death with out even a chance to live once they are born. Is this the new thinking of Obama and Nancy Pelosi Government are they turning the United States of America into a Country of legal murders. If Pelosi and Obama can do that and get these laws passed with no opposition and not even the main stream news media saying this is wrong and the People of this Country to sit on their hands and not do nothing to stop these murders. Where are the mothers to cry out to stop murdering babies. Doesn't Pelosi see the blood on her hands. Obama is also a cold blooded killer of life. These murders will go on for years to come if it isn't stopped. Is the Pelosi, Obama, Socialist Democrat party line murder babies and that is more important than life itself.

If we the people can sit back and allow the Government to pass legal murder laws when will they pass laws that it is right and just to murder children who's learning skills are not up to what Government say they should be. What will stop the new Obama Socialist Government from condemning anyone for that matter if their eyes are not the right color if they may be short in size, if Nancy Pelosi and Obama can control the Congress to pass a law with to murder babies they can pass a law to murder anyone for any reason they can think of. Too many people living in the world, the United States has to take the lead and every second person, in that household, of any age in that comes up the Government data base has to die. But they who make these laws they and their friends and families are exempt from being put to death because it is Politically right.

What is the difference between Obama, Nancy Pelosi and the new Socialist Democratic Party. They are worried about Gay Rights, Civil Rights, Terrorist rights at Gitmo who have no rights because they are not citizens of the United states and the enemy of the United States taken prisoner during a war. The Socialist Obama Government are concerned with illegal aliens rights, every group of humans rights, BUT NOT RIGHTS OF BABIES WHO WILL BE MURDERED BECAUSE WOMEN ARE USING ABORTION AS A FORM OF BIRTH CONTROL.

We the people have to flood the Liberal Socialist Congress with phone calls and e-mails and letters everyday telling the all the Baby Killers that these innocent children deserve the RIGHT TO LIVE, not only by the Constitution but by GOD"S LAW.

Where is the Pope telling the people what the should do? Where are all the leaders of the Judeo/ Christian Churches telling there flock that if they believe in GOD they should fight for the right of these poor little souls to live THE AMERICAN WAY.

Do you think that if we, the people who believe in God do nothing to stop these murders by law, we are also guilty of murder, along with the Godless Obama, Nancy Pelosi the leader of the murdering Socialist Democrats in Congress. We are 300,000,000 people who are going to let 500, Godless people tell us that it is OK to commit murder under the LAW of the United States of America. Yes we can stop them, we can drive these killers out of Congress by telling them that they are guaranteed that they will not be elected on the next election, even if Obama's ACORN radicals try and seal the vote as they have done in his Presidential election. Stop by the Main Stream News Media's News papers, tell the sponsors of the main stream

TV station sponsors that we will not buy their products if they support Obama murder program of killing babies, take away their money and they will turn on Obama, Nancy Pelosi and the Socialist Democratic Party in fact the Democratic Killers will devourer themselves all we have to do is e-mail, write letters that fill the Congress and Senate Floors and fill the rooms with protest papers. We do not need some one to lead us to stop these unnecessary murders of innocent babies, we are our own leaders, do not believe in man believe in yourself.

Wake up America.

Who created the Council on Foreign Relations

In 1921 Edward M. House formed the Council on Foreign Relations, which even though it sounds like it might part of the Federal Government, it is not. Form the very start of the Council on Foreign Relations it's only purpose was to destroy the United States of America. Colonel House was never in the armed forces that were the "nick name he was given by those around him because he was a strong arm guy, the same as Rom Emmanuel is for Obama.

From the start of Council on Foreign Relations, the men of that time who were in power and influence in Wall Street and Banks, J.P. Morgan, Rockefeller and others, who financed the Council, have moved to destroy the United States of America and take it over themselves. By gaining foot holds in all parts of Government, the domination over the State Department was one and the Council has controlled it ever since. To keep this control the Council has contributed millions of dollars to Presidents, Congressmen and Senators Campaigns, they hold a great amount of influence over these people who we voted for to run the Government. When I say contributed to their campaigns, in realty it's called a bribe to do the biding of the Council when they tell their Congressmen and Senators and Presidents what they want them to do.

The Council on Foreign Relations is a rich Elitist group of Marxist thinking men in the World. They actually want to destroy the sovereignty of the United States of America, with the help of Obama and Tim Geithner well on the way to Bankrupting the Country the Council on Foreign Relations are close to that objective. Tim Geithner holds a high position in the Council on Foreign Relations and also knows the President of the New York Federal Reserve Bank who is an associate of the governor of the Chinese central bank, who Geithner has been helping China with their investments in the American stock market, Geithner also speaks fluent Chinese, one of the main reasons Obama and Gang picked Geithner. This is today, now and is one of the reasons Geithner and Obama robbed the Treasury, also Obama taking his orders from the Council on Foreign Relations among other in influential think tanks wanting to destroy America. All that Obama has done in a few months has been waiting for him, because everyone, for the first time, is in place to destroy the United States of America it was all written out before Obama became President, all he had to do is be the "Front Man.

All of this is not only leading to bankrupting America and America loosing its sovereignty and The New World Order. The New World Order comes in with the Trilateral Commission that was started by David Rockefeller and Zbigniew Brzezinski, who worships Marxism, like House became the influential mind controlling person who controlled and taught Jimmy Carter of the New World Order. We can see how Carter runs all over the Mid-East talking to our enemies, al Qaida, and other terrorist groups pretending that his speaking for the people of the United States and the Government. Carter like Obama thinks that they are the rulers of the World.

All the Presidents since Carter filled all the administrative posts with people from the Council on Foreign Relations and The Trilateral Commission. We the American citizen do not realize it but our Government is controlled by quite a few institutions, we think that everything is on the up and up with our Government but it is not. Like the Federal Government giving money to Banks and taking over Gm or what eve Company takes money for them they now own them and they have to do what the Government says to they have to do, so works The Council on Foreign Relations and George Soros and many more. Look at Joe Biden, Vice President, the News Media has never said anything about who Joe Biden has been taking money form for many years and it goes into the millions, Iran. Biden does what Iran tells him to do. The news media is controlled by The Council on Foreign Relations.

The Council on Foreign Relations is one of the reasons we fight wars where we don't belong and we loose, because that is the way The Council on Foreign relations wants it to be. Why do you think Obama leans toward Cuba, all of South America and is not happy with the military coup that took place in Honduras, and ousted their Marxist President who like Obama, Chavez, and Castro wants to be dictators for life, because he is like all these people.

The real goal of The Council on Foreign Relations, The Trilateral, do you remember when George Bush Senior broke the news to the United States that when he promised us the New World Order. This is what the real New World Order means, Our Government leaders Obama and his Gang are following through with the "Plan". Why do you think they are all stealing all the money they can get their hands on? Why do you think that Obama opened the gates to the Lobbyists after promising the people there would be no more Lobbyists, they walk into the white House to see Obama it costs them $5,000.00 every time, nice piece of chump change that goes right into Obama's pocket. The United States is being made into a carbon copy of a Communist State. Then all the Marxist Countries can merge together and create a New World Order where only the rich rule, and we the people become slaves to our new rulers.

How can we beat these evil money hungry leaders? We have to pray to God to help us win our Freedom from all these people and the next thing is don't ever let the Government take away your right to own and use a gun. Because if America looses the Second Amendment when the New World Order takes over we will see a mass murder of the America people that will make Hitler's murder of the Jews look like it was nothing. If you don't think that will happen here think again. Obama like House and The council on Foreign Relations care less if we Americans live or die. Obama is committed to the murder of at least 45,000 babies a year and with his health care plan that Obama wants he will kill 100,000 more people because you will not be able to get the medical you need to live. The President and the Congress and the Senate have already passed a bill that exempts them and their families from Universal Health Care, they and their families will always get the best health care over the American Citizen. That's how Marxism works. Take a look at how

Obama and his Gang operate. His wife went to France and England on a shopping trip. While we are being told that we have to sacrifice our way of life and lower our standard of living they live like Kings. Don't believe the News Media because it is controlled by The Council on Foreign Relations. Look it up. We the tax payers pay for it all even the what ever they want to buy.

Antonio Gramsci's disciple Barrack Hussain Obama

Following Antonio Gramsci's Marxist formula to the letter, which Russia has also adopted, to destroy the United States of America. By bankrupting the Country, is just one way to destroy the American people. One of the main things that Obama has to do and he is getting plenty of help from the ACLU, who go to the supreme court and work against the values of Americans and tears down anything that looks like Christianity in the United States. Obama takes a lot of orders from the Institute for Policy Studies, who have a direct line to Russia, along with the National Lawyers Guild, Center for Constitutional Rights and many more organizations that are in the mix to destroy the United States of America. With the Congressional Progressive Caucus which has been in place for years, Pelosi was the Chairman at one time until she was elected Chairman of the House where she can really do a lot of damage to the people of the

United States and our freedom. The 77 members of the Congressional Progressive Caucus control most of the voting in Congress. And none of these people are for the United States of America. They also take their orders from the Institute for Policy Studies, is a Russian Satellite in America.

Why is Obama's focus going around the Europeans, the Muslims and all the Nations south of the Border? Now as Obama sees things from his quote to the Muslim World, "America is not a religious Country they, not we, are only Citizens...? So what is he telling the World, do not believe in God, or your Religion, believe in Man, and they must believe in Obama because he can go into the World and solve all the problems, he, Obama is more powerful than God. All the problems of the World were created by Man and a Man, Obama has only to talk to people and they will do what ever he says. Obama can talk to North Korea and tell them to stop their development of nuclear weapons, since Obama let the World know that he is cutting back on the defense system of this Country North Korea has gone ahead at full throttle with their nuclear rockets and tests. North Korea has even threatened to declare war on any Country that tried to stop him, meaning the United States of America. Obama is afraid, to stop one of North Korea 's ships that the United States suspects has more nuclear hard wear on it that was shipped out of China. Obama in one of his brilliant speeches that would lull North Korea to sleep and roll over and say Obama is our leader, didn't work.

Obama is trying to take the place of God to the Muslims World had Iran believe what he said, which was basically freedom from tyranny and that he would back them up. As usual in his abstract speeches you believe what you think Obama said and not what he really said. Obama led the Iranian people believe that if they revolted against Ahamadinejad, that Obama would step in and help them over throw the yoke of tyranny. Obama will not go against the real ruler of Iran Ayatollah Ali Khamenei who is supreme word of the Koran and Obama has always said he was for the Muslims. Now these Iranians believed Obama in his speech that he and he alone, don't even think to pray to God because he is the new Man God who can solve all the Worlds ills.

That is one of the parts of the Gramsci creeds, Man is now God, and Obama is practicing how to look like the Marxist god of the World.

It is too bad that we Americans think that if we don't do anything to save our freedom our free-dom will be saved. Americans better get up from behind the TV and beer and start getting involved in who they vote for, Americans better smarten up soon before they wake up one morning and there is no America. You can't trust the News Media at all. They are State run with disinformation and propaganda for Obama and the Marxist take over.

Democrats and Republicans wrecking U.S. civilization

We the people of the United States of America are being pushed back into the Dark Ages by the very same people who we voted for to keep our County free and moving forward going into the 21st Century, where we should be living the really good life. By that I mean no worries about making a good living, having a nice home, a car that would give you 5 hundred horse power and 5 hundred miles to a gallon of gas, cures for heart problems, cancer you name it and we the people would have it, we wouldn't be in wars we are not supposed to win, that last for ten years or more killing our children.

For the last one hundred years the starting Woodrow Wilson, the supreme elitist at the beginning of the twentieth century our Congressmen and Senators have worked against the people of the United States to bring us to where we are now on the brink of Communism, and only for their welfare. With the coming of 2006 Democrats have now captured both the Congress and the Senate, plus the Presidency. The Communist Democrats and Republicans are now poised to stab the United States in the back, with the take over of the Banks the car industry, and now health care. When the Federal Government put interfere with the natural order of society they go out of their way destroy it.

With the Government taking over our health care and they are putting everyone's name into a computer system that will tell the operator every detail of your life and they will now control every thing you do. Also with this health care there will be no more advancement in the medical field Medical field for cures of cancer, heart, or any other disease because 545 people think that they know best how you should live your life and they are going to put into law. With Obama/Pelosi/ Reid, and all the Communist Democrats and Republicans in charge of the United States of America we will move backwards to the dark ages.

There has never been a time, from Wilson's Presidency that our Federal Government have not wanted to take over. It started small a hundred years ago to right now at this moment 2010. These

2,000 word bills that nobody wants to read and they are made that long so no one will read them ,have been around for a long time just waiting for the moment in history for the destruction and take over of the United States, every thing is in place, people and money. Our Presidents and Congressmen and Senators have written laws that hurt the average America citizen. They created taxes that we can't afford, they have created Racism, where one group is preferred over another, weather they qualify for a job or getting into a college it's a bad law, Affirmative Action, that doesn't bring the Country together, they have successfully split the Country. Will they resend that law, no.

We now have Multiculturalism, no more one people in a Nation, look at the Black Caucus and the Latino Caucus even though these people were born in the United States of America they do not conceder themselves American. The Black Caucus conceder themselves Africans and the Latino's conceder themselves Mexican, Puerto Rican, Cuban but not American, German, Polish, Italian, Irish and on and on. They do not work for the good of all the people they work for the good of their people.

There is very little loyalty to America and who caused this, the Federal Government. Becoming a two language Country, our Congressmen and Senators caused this with the stroke of a pen, they split the Country in half again, remember this one, United we stand Divided we fall. These things have not happened over night. There are plans for the future that Nations make called the 50 year plan or a 100 year plan what ever it takes to do what ever the Controllers of mankind want. And these people through generation after generation have worked to this end. Our Presidents and Congressmen complain abut high taxes and inflation, they are the cause of it. When they run for reelection they all campaign for lower taxes, but the taxes keep getting higher and higher, and we the dummies keep electing the same people over and over. Then they try and make you believe it is your fault, but the people don't have control over the laws the Congressmen and Senators do. With Obama and all the Communist Democrats and Republicans we are going backwards, our standard of living is going down again. We are being punished by the Federal Government to satisfy, Europe and the UN?

Another point being is the Communist President Obama and the Communist Democrats and Republicans will always have the best of everything we the people will not, and with ACORN, the Unions and amnesty for millions of Illegal Mexicans they are guaranteed their positions for the rest of their lives and this will make way for their children to step into their Congressional and Senatorial seats. This is what the Congressmen and

Senators who are in Obama's club want, all the Democrats will soon never have to worry about an election again. In fact they will change the law and no one will stop them, there will be no more free elections no elections at all and they will be there in those Congressional and Senate sets for ever, ruling us with an iron fist. If you think that Hitler Stalin and all the Dictators of the modern and old worlds murdered their own people like they do in Africa, Obama Pelosi/Reid Communist Government will commit atrocities to the people of the United States that you cannot imagine.

This along with the Obama health care plan will throw us back to the time when the kings, prince's dukes and earls who ruled the kingdoms. Why do you think the politicians are stealing so much our tax payer dollars, because when they collapse our economy to zero and we loose our sovereignty they will be extremely rich and be ready for the "New World Order", UN "One World Government," This is where they will tell you if or if you can live or die, weather you can have children. Weather they can learn to read and write. We will all be brain washed by the Communist State to think like a zombie, act like a zombie and only be allowed to live because they will have to serve their masters, to worship our savior Obama and the Communist Democrats and Republicans who destroyed America. This already being done starting in the public schools where the children are taught songs of the great World Savior Barrack Husain Obama, And is it stopped, I don't think so, because the State run news media also agree with this. So do the educators from grammar school to and through college; if you don't believe this read David Horowitz's book, One Party Classroom and get sick to your stomach, because this is where you are sending your children to get brain washed to turn against you and the United States of America, and become Racists, hate the white people, hate, hate freedom and love Marxism, hate the rich because that is what they teach.

Do you think that for minute these morons that we have elected to run our Country and keep us free write these 2,000 page laws that secretly destroy our Constitution along with our freedom, no they are not. They have done everything in their power to wreck the USA. It appears that every law that they pass is written by a Communist think tanks, in Washington DC. Think tanks like the Institute for State Policy, Rand, Brookings Institute, and friends of Obama, Robert Kramer who wrote a book while in prison that Obama says is the rule of thumb that Pelosi/Reid and the Communist Democrats and Republicans will follow as a guide line to bring Communism into being, this guy sat in jail and wrote guide lines how to wreck this Country. Obama quote. "judge me by the people I surround my self with" Communists, liars, cheats and big time thieves. So what does that tell us about Obama? Every time we elect some a person to any office we are giving over to them our rights and freedom to do what they want, not what we want.

Our Government has and is right at this moment bringing our standard of living down lower then it has ever been, by taxing us to death, and that is only one way. Has anyone noticed that the price of food is going higher and higher every day, that gasoline is staying at $2.50 and going higher and it is not going down That Louis Gutierrez and Nancy Pelosi who told the illegal emigrants on notional TV that it is unconstitutional that they have to live in the United States in fear that they will be deported and that she and Gutierrez are going to make sure they get amnesty and a free ride. They get that now. Do you think that Pelosi, Gutierrez are really thinking of these people, yes they are, not because they feel sorry for them, but because they will be a bigger base for their votes. They did the same thing with the Black community by Government subsidizing them, they now control their votes. It is all about money and power, and the people are the slaves to Government.

The Communist Democrats are already starting to cheat by passing a law by Barney. Frank, to register everyone every one who owns a driver license, is collecting Compensation from the Government, who is receiving aid from the Govern-

ment, and Frank and the Communist Congressmen and Senators will use any dishonest way to
bring all these voters forward to make sure that
only Communist/Marxist/ and moron Democrats
get elected. This way anyone with the help of their
Percent Captains can vote as many times as are
told, or steal an election like they did in Minnesota, where votes found in the trunk of car, 10,000,
after the election was counted for the biggest
clown in the USA, to help wreck our Country. The
it used to be before the coming of Obama, the
polls opened at 7:00 A.M and closed at 6:00 P.M.
any vote that wasn't counted on the day of election were not counted, who or what organization
gave the order to the Minnesota politicians the
order to count these bogus votes so Al the clown
Franklin would win that senate seat for the Progressive Communist Democrats.

You must they denounce the rich as the bad
guys but in reality they are the Super rich!!

Bureaucracies in place in America

Here is a great example of Bureaucracy pork that really does no good to keep America safe from terrorists crossing our borders or checking our airports. The United States must have at least 30 government police agencies working through out the United States of America. They cost the American tax payers millions if not billions dollars a year and then there is their pension funds that we the tax payer have to foot the bill. An example ,why can't say the Chicago Police Department keep tabs on Midway and O'Hara airports they have always watched the airports and everything else. Take a look at Jimmy Carters energy bureaucracy that was supposed to get us off foreign oil and discover ways to be our own energy producing Country. They have been a bureaucracy for more than thirty years and it costs we tax payers 43 billions dollars a year to support this in house pork Bureaucracy, have they done their job finding better ways to get us off foreign oil. NO! They just waste tax payers money. They must employ a thousand people or more. We are more dependent on foreign oil now more than we ever were. And of course we shouldn't forget that Jimmy Carter sold the Panama Canal to China our enemy. Or we shouldn't forget Bill Clinton help sell our oil fields in Alaska to England. Now if push comes to shove and England says America can't have any of this oil we are out of luck. I wonder how much of a kick back the Clintons got for that one.

Once a Bureaucracy or give away program is in place Marxist Democrats and Republicans never shut it down even if it is breaking the back of America and causing the American people to pay more taxies. Look what our Marxists Government has done to Social Security, this one from our first real Marxist President Jimmy Carter, if a person comes into this Country from another Country legally or illegally and he or she is 65 or older that person will receive at least 2,000.00 dollars a month with out never having to work a single day in their life. But if you are a Citizen of the United States born and raised here and a veteran and you worked all your life in the Social Security system you will be lucky to get 750.00 a month and you can't complain about it. You can go to your Congressmen or Senator and you will get nowhere. Then our Marxist Democrats and Republicans have a couple more give away programs of our tax dollars not theirs they get to keep all their money, bought salary and bribes, which run into the millions and they don't even have to pay tax on anything, and if they are caught, like a few just recently they get a pass they don't even have to pay a penalty, Tim Geithner for one, and he got to be the head of the IRS and the Treasury, how about that American Tom Daschle, he didn't get the job, good thing because he wrote the book on how not to give the American public any medical aid which we all paid for when we paid into Social Security all our lives. Daschle worked for Medical Insurance Companies while he was an elected official and took their money by the bushel full to help them, not you, and now he works for them now as a lobbyist making a couple million a year to bribe his friends in the Senate and the Congress to work against the American tax payer.

Our Marxist Democrats and Republicans have always, since Affirmative Action was put into law all the Black community not only get a free college education but they also get free housing, in Chicago a Black student can apply for and get free housing in any building that has renters and Condos they can be moved in for free, because these builders took Marxist Federal money, Government control in action. Now that we have millions of illegal Mexicans in the United States they get free education, free hospitalization, free money to help support their families and they also qualify for Affirmative Action because they are classed as Black. If Barrack Hessian Obama puts any Bureaucracy into place, watch out for Socialized Medicine at least a minimum of 75,000 people a year will die because you won't be able to get the health care you need. The United States of America will be thrown back 300 years. Everyone who is not an American Citizen will be taken care of first. As an American Citizen a senior you will not get the care because some Marxist Bureaucrat sitting in some building will be charge of your life and I guarantee you will die by their decision. He will look at the Medical Book of rules of who should be taken care of and who should not. It will read something like this if the person is, 55 or older he or she will not get medical attention because they should die soon with in a few years, why keep them healthy?

WAKE UP AMERICA, Obama is a killer of mankind any one who can condemn 50,000 innocent babies, just in the United States alone, and send money to other Countries to help kill their innocent babies, what makes you think he has feelings for any human being on this earth let alone in the World. He is and claims to be the new god of the Marxist Democrats and Republicans and the World. .

None of these things are good for all of Americans and the Marxist Democrats and Republicans will never take them away, they never have and they never will. Only the American Citizen will suffer and complain sitting around with his friend's having a beer but will never do anything to stop the abuse, until it hurts him then he or she will cry out for Justice and their will be none, because it is to late. They should have thought about who they were voting for before they voted.

A Democrat Marxist Leveling the Playing Field
By Douglas Dauntless

This is what the people of the United States have to look forward too. The Marxist Democrats that are running this Country have just showed what the Obama, Soros, Pelosi, Reid, Durbin, the whole crew of Elitists who have now taken over the Government mean when they talk about the "Poor'. The poor Blacks of the United States or in the World, have it better than any working man no matter what color he is. They get a free ride, they live better, they have 50' plasma TVs in their homes, I have seen them driving around in new BMW"S and Mercedes, they make tons of tax free money on the side. The only poor who are not doing well are the drug addicts' the Marxist Obama Democrats using the "Poor" to get to be the wealthiest people in the World.

Now comes what Obama and the Marxists Democrats call leveling the playing field, they must have been taught by Vladimir Putin when he first took office, he did exactly what Obama, Pelosi, Reid, Franks, and Dodd did they broke the Banking system and then blamed Wall Street. Obama, Clinton Marxist then put the United States into Trillions of dollars of debt. They hurt the working man and will destroy the Middle-Class which is what Obama was always after, and while doing this the Elitists Marxist Democrats became millionaires over night and some Dianne Feinstein, Obama, Biden, Pelosi, Franks, Dodd, and Reid have become billionaires over night. Senator Dianne Feinstein made sure that her husband got a 25 billion dollar, up front contract from her Marxist Democrats and made sure she and her family will remain part of the richest people in the World. Corruption is the key to the Obama Marxist Government. As the Obama Marxist Democrats level the playing field they will be sure to make sure that the free people of the United States will have their property and businesses taken away from them by the resent law passed by the Supreme Court called EMENT DOMAIN, which means the Government has the right to take away what you own, but Obama and the Corrupt Marxist will not redistribute the wealth they will keep for themselves. The whole working Middle-Class and anyone who works will be poor having to live on handouts by the Elite Marxist Democrats. They the Elitists Marxist will live like the Kings of the World and we the people will live no better than the poorest Country in the world. Now will come the executions of millions of Americans who did not agree with the Obama Marxist Dogma. There will be no law but the Marxist Obama law, their will be no Police but the Marxist Obama Police, and they will be the Gangbangers who now roam the Cities and streets of the United States and are free to do as they please. Our Armed forces will be turned over to the UN, we will have no more sons to fight for the freedom of America. We will not be able to fight for our freedom because right now as I write this Eric Holder is plotting how to disarm the law abiding citizens of the United States of America. The Obama Marxist Congress knows that the people of the United States will not give up there freedoms. The Obama Marxist Democrats and Republicans are afraid of a real live Rebellion because of the destruction to the United States Obama is causing. We will be ruled by the Marxist Elite Democrats and there will never be an honest election with the Obama army in place called ACORN to steal the votes for other Marxists Democrats and Republicans.

The Main- Stream News Media will not challenge anything Obama wants to do even if it is against the laws of the Constitution of the United States of America.

Obama is more Corrupt than anyone in the History of the United States, he is a true traitor to the United States he has sold us out to every European Country he has visited and sold us and Israel out to the Muslims, and now recently to Castro, Chavez, and da Silva. Why would he just sit at this summit and listen to these Pan- American Countries tear the United States apart and not stand up for the United States of America, because he hates everything about America, it's wealth, it's laws, it's freedoms, it's Middle-Class working people, any one who tries to get ahead by starting their own business, he hates our Soldiers more than the Clintons do, he loves the enemies of the United States.

You want to see what real Marxism and communism is look to Cuba, Venezuela, and the Countries that Chavez and Castro are converting over to Marxism with the same false promise of the Gramsci' Marxist World take care of the poor. Obama acts as if he really knows what he is doing, he doesn't have a clue, all these things have been thought out for him to do by the Clintons, Pelosi, Soros, Reid and the Marxist think tanks in Washington DC. All Obama thinks is that he is the god of the World and he can do no wrong, everyone will do as he says. Remember in leveling the playing field of the American people he will make every one poor. You will never be able to see a Doctor, or you will never have a choice of what religion you want to belong to or a free choice of anything you might want. More than likely we'll be forced to turn to his religion of choice the Muslim Religion. You will have no choice how you want to raise or educate your children. We got a good look at how the Government wants to raise and educate your children when another Elitist Marxist, do as I say and not as I do, Al Gore when on national television he told the children of the United States not to listen to their parents because parents are out of touch with the Marxist World Gore belongs to.

The Obama Marxist Home land security have no right to call any American who attends a tea party or protests Obama in any way, because right now we have the right to protest the Government, and the Main-Stream News Media has a lot of nerve to call the tea parties racist because there were no Black people their. If the Black community didn't want to show up it is because of their Black Nationalist Attitude of their own Racist ideas for the White community. This is what Americas future is going to be for us. They. Obama, Clintons, Pelosi. Feinstein, and the Elite Marxist Democrats live the great life we the people will live like dogs.

Once all these things are in place then the Murders began, by Law, Obama's Law!

Wake up America!!

Donate to me and I will save you

Lately I have been getting US mail and e-mail from Congressmen and Senators, Democrat and Republicans asking for donations, also from the Democratic and Republican Parties. In the name of anything why should I or anyone of us give these Senators and Congressmen money to save us from the new Obama/Pelosi/ Reid Communist Democrats or Republicans? They are all millionaires or like Dianne Feinstein, Nancy Pelosi, Reid, Frank, Dodd, Murtaugh, Obama, Biden we can't forget Hillary Clinton or any of them. With the help of Obama and Geitner they just robbed the treasury and cut up the money.

They get millions of dollars from defense contractors, except Dianne Feinstein's husband, they give him more contracts for anything under the sun that she can think of. Pelosi is the same she works for the more riches for her husband all with our tax dollars than she works for the people of the United States. We are forced to pay unjust taxes or the United States Gestapo, the IRS will come and take everything you own and still charge you a, what should we call it...a late fee that will double what you owe to the IRS. Do they care if you can survive after that, no they don't, all it means is that our trusted Senators and Congressmen can steal more from us. It is their right as Senators and Congressmen for having been voted into office by us. Let's take a look at Joe Biden, when you see him you think this guy is a wise intelligent man. No he is not he is no smarter than you or I, what he or any of them do, we the common people can to do the same job, more then likely better than they can. Joe Biden for years has been taking money form one of Americas enemies, and the money goes into the millions, from Iran. Obama just gave him $25,000,000.00 dollars to renovate the train station he used to go to work from. More than likely he had a relative bid on the contract to rebuild this station and they cut up the money between them, they probably did do some renovating that cost a couple million but that's about all. Now his son wants to run for Congressmen or Senator, keep it in the family, like the Kennedys. They see the millions of dollars that their parents get away with and they are schooled by them how to lie cheat and steal the tax payers money because the tax payers are dummies they will let them get away with anything, and the people are dummies for voting for the Party not the person and for these same people over and over again so they get more power and more power they can commit treason against the USA and no will stop them, all they have to do is cut up the money. Look at Congressmen Rangel, he gets away with stealing and not paying his taxes because first of all he is sitting in Nancy Pelosi's pocket and second of all because he is Black and that is his pay back for the way white people treated the Black people. But Rangel and Pelosi have cut a ton of money between them, how can she turn on her partner in legalized crime against the people of the United States. None of them pay their taxes until they are caught and then it's not much even though under the table they may owe $10,000,000.00 in back taxes but that's OK they are only working for the people. The only reason the Rangel and the other Black Congressmen and Senators get in is because the Black communities know what ever it is that you do as long as you are Black it is OK. These men and women rob from them, they cheat them out of their hard earned dollars, for those that work and they keep voting them in over and over. I have never seen a Black leader in my life help any one but themselves; a good example of this is Jessie Jackson Jr, and the other son that Jackson threatened Bud Wiser with a Black boycott, Bud Wiser caved in and gave his son a Bud Wiser Distributorship in the heart of Chicago for free.

Another good example is Senator Chambliss of the Great State of Georgia has played golf all over the United States for years and some outside the United States and paid over $200,000.00 just to pay golf the money comes from donations by lobbyists and some of it comes from his expense account paid by us, I am sure that he had to take his wife with him, they go first class and live first class and eat first class and I am sure that he invites a friend or two that we pay for. Where is this guy looking out for the American people? We have to save for years just to take our kids to Disney for a week and go into debt,. These Senators and Congressmen have a well of money so deep it has no bottom. I listened to one of his speeches last year and in a treble voice he yelled about going green and doing something about being sure that Ethanol will be the fuel of the feature, you know whose pocket he is sitting in. They are liars' crooks and thieves, grabbing all the money they can while they can, because when they get knocked out by the voters they get their full salary for the rest of their lives and if they die their family gets the money for rest of their lives.

Becoming a Politian is the only business in the World that you can go into poor and come so rich that it is unbelievable, to never have to worry about being poor again or going to jail while you are committing crimes and treason against the United States of America's people. A brainless person who used to be friend told me he was voting for Obama because he was going to tax the rich, I told him, you and people like us are the rich, he will never tax the rich they only tax the working man, then he said I am going to vote for Hillary Clinton she a tough broad, Hillary Clinton caved into her new lord and master Barrack Hussein Obama, when he told her in his Chicago accent get out in the street in Florida Hillery and work for me, now. And away she went. So much for being tough.

So here we are the Greatest Free Country in the World going into a Communist World led by 500 people who control the laws of the land. Three hundred million America Citizens can't stop them, because they refuse to listen to us. It is our own fault we have let them lie, cheat steal, and commit every crime you can think of against us and we did not stop them. One reason they make sure that the Country is run in Chaos, all the problems we have today and yesterday were and have been caused by these Politian's and then they tell us they will solve the problems they caused every problem we have, Wars that we are not allowed to win, Racism, Banks going under, Foreign Countries coming into this Country and buying up everything in site. Saudi Arabia owns 8% of the United States, Germany owns a ton of farm land that they harvest and take back to Germany. Our standard of living is in the basement. There are certain groups of people that were sacrificed for another race that would make them equal, it didn't work that group of people have become more savage than any other group in the USA, except the Mexican 13 Gangs because laws were passed to let them loose on society. Obama is building his own Army it's called the Green Army; they are being trained to take over the streets. It is against the Constitution of the United States. Where our great Senators and Congressmen to stop this are, they are nowhere they are part of it. Where is the Supreme Court, Where are the Checks and balances? Never give up your gun for no one not even this Country. We will need them if we are going to survive, because by November 2010 Obama and his Communist Democrats and Republicans, and their Republican leader John McCain will be too late, they can and will cause so much damage to our freedom and our Country that we will have to fight and die for our Country and our Freedom. And these phonies still want us to give them money from our hard earned money to help them get re-elected to help destroy our Country, our Freedom, commit Treason and any other crime against us.

God has Blessed America other wise we would have been destroyed a long time ago by our Communist Democrats and Republicans. Now God is asking the people who listen that we should make a stand with Him against Barrack Hussein

Obama and Nancy Pelosi, Reid and all the rest of these Traitors against God and our Freedom. We the people who believe in the United States of America are going to have fight and die for America if we want to be Free.

Dumbing Down
12/03/10

Glenn Beck coined the phrase on his TV show the other night I thought about it and he is right. The Progressive elite Democrats and Republicans and all the super-elites that are not in Government who think that they are the chosen one's to not only run the United States into the ground and rule the world, they do not want the real people of the United States to raise above a laborer status or a gorilla mentality so the people do not become a threat to our rulers. i.e. the progressive Democrats and Republicans leveling the playing field forcing us into the "Dark Ages" where we only existed to serve those who ruled the land, Kings, Princes, Earls, Dukes and so on.

The Progressives, Laura Bush and George who put into action "No Child Left Behind", sounds wonderful, your children are going to get a brake. No it doesn't work that way. There are children who are extremely intelligent who will be left behind because they are not allowed to use their God given intelligence to move forward and pass the class that they are in, to move ahead with their intelligence, they are forced to stay in a class where it moves along so slowly they have to keep up with the slowest minds in the class. That is not fare to those children who are more intelligent. These children will stop using their brains and wind up bored and hateing school and education all their lives. Thus the Elites successfully shutting the brains down so that our children will never become leaders in the United States, their will never be new inventions to move mankind forward again like Henry Ford, Thomas Elision. These things are only allowed for the Elites children not for the regular man's children who are smarter then the Elites children. The Elites children are only smart because of their parent's station in life that will move them forward but they will not contribute to the good of man kind they will only contribute to the good of their own kind.

"No Child Left Behind" is a lie. There are children who need special care because of some physical defect in their bodies, these poor children need more help then say a normal physically OK child. Some of these poor children are extremely intelligent and they could advance quickly, but they will be held back and Dumb Down. Then there are children who are just normal intelligent who are being Dumbed Down. The Elites are depending on stupidity and ignorance to win out. They want slaves to come into being in the United States to serve them. They tried it with the Black Community by Dumbing them down, because the Progressives Democrats and Republicans have no respect for them, they only want their votes, which they get because of the hand outs they give them. Now the Mexicans are going to be their new slaves, they come here already with a slave mentality because all their lives they have been raised in ignorance, so the Progressives are doing the same thing to them and they will be preferred over the Black community as the new Progressive Democrat voting block. But in the mean time the hand outs are coasting the working man billions of dollars in tax money that should be going to take care of America but it is not. There are people on welfare that are collecting hundreds of thousand dollars in welfare, and that includes all the Muslims who have four wives all their children get $1,500 a month per child. That is one of the reasons the Elites do not want your children, mostly white children to get ahead. This is not Racism this is a fact. Everything that the Progressive Democrats and Republicans have done is to destroy the White population and keep them dumb, how best to do this is through education from the very start.

Extremely interesting, the people we are helping to fight off, with money and arms and anything else you can think of sell all we give them to fight the entire Jihadist in Iraq and Afghanistan or anywhere else the Presidents, and the UN decide to send our children to get killed and mangled for nothing, our allies sell all our weapons and equipment to the enemy who then turn those American made weapons on our troops and kill and wound them. We give them money to help support our troops they keep the money and become rich over the bodies of our Children that our stupid Presidents and Congressmen and Senators send there to die.

All the people in the Middle East are all Muslim, they all belong to the Muslim Religion, they have been fighting each other for a thousand years, and they all belong to the Muslim Brother Hood, run by Saudi Arabia, another friend and enemy at the same time. The two Bush Presidents and now Obama are owned by the Saudis. Muslims are required by to speak the truth with other believers, but not to none believers, that's the law of the Koran.

Muslims can be friendly non Muslims but they cannot be friends. That means that they, according to their religion they can lie cheat, steal, and even help the enemy fight and kill our soldiers for their cause to convert the World to Islam. Our children are there not to win the freedom of the

Afghan or Iraqi people they are there to die for nothing. There are no enemies among the Muslims, they are all the same. This hundred years the Taliban win, the next hundred years the Sunni win. The United States will not win; we will lose and become more weakened with not enough man power to keep America free and running, also the all the Politian's have nothing to worry about because the competition is being killed off. This also fits in with the Obama plan of weakening he kills all the babies he can, Obama does not want to take care of the military that are wounded, Obama will be able to save millions of dollars if the Military die, as with his Medicare plan to kill off millions of seniors.

I read this article and it got me thinking. From the end of WWII, the United States has gotten involved in Korea, not by us declaring war, because that Country attacked us, but because of our Presidents signing alliances with a particular Country, but most often or not we send our children into harms way because of the UN.

Korea, a UN war, who sent the most troops and supplied almost all of the supplies, the United States did. We lost 40,000,000 or 50,000,000 young men average age 18 to 25, for what? To fight Communism, to fight for Korea's freedom from Communism, to fight for the UN, to what end. The United States was not supposed to win that War or Police Action as it was called. Then why were we and other Countries their, why did we have to have more men then any other Country. The powers that caused this War to happen keep weakening our Country by killing off our youth, most of them were white. These young men who died for nothing would have married and had children and populate the United States and keep it solvent and strong. These young men were sacrificed like lambs going to the slaughter. We did not win the Korean War because we were not meant to win the war, it was settled to cut the Country in half at the 38th parallel. No win!

Looking at Obama, who is a cold blooded killer of mankind and reading about the Council on Foreign Relations, which is not a Federal Government organization, but made up of some of the wealthiest people, like David Rockefeller, world banks, and almost all of our politicians, along with the Trilateral Commission, the Builderburgs, and again there are our politicians right in with them working to destroy the United States of America. Obama is going to send in thousands of our children to fight in Afghanistan, a UN war and he is going to cut the defense budget that will help get more of our children killed, to protect the poppy fields for some big shot in the UN that wants to control all the dope in the world. Where are the people to stop Obama and the Politicians, where are the big shot movie stars to protest the Meddle-

East Wars? They are no where in sight because they love Obama and his gang of cutthroats and want to see America die like Jane Fonda, who screamed at a group of College graduates, "get down on your knees and pray that you become a Communist" it doesn't hurt her she's rich and will not have to suffer, like all the disloyal movie stars.

Let's look at Viet Nam. Another War that killed thousands of young men because the President signed a Gulf of Token alliance with Indo-China as it was called at the time. The United States supplied almost all of the troops, and supplies to the South Viet Nam and their leaders stole the money and kept it and then helped the enemy then helped the enemy by selling them our arms to kill our soldiers. There were a lot of sincere Viet Nam people that in the end were left behind to die. Again the United States was not supposed to win that war either; we stayed there for over seven years letting our children die for nothing. But I am sure that our Presidents and Congressmen, Senators both men and women made small fortunes from this war by being able to secure million dollar military and civilian contracts from the panels they sat on, just like Dianne Feinstein, Nancy Pelosi, Franks, Dodd, and all of them do right now. What happened in the Viet Nam War, The "hate your Country, hate the Armed forces, College Professors and the Main Stream News Media along with the Jane Fonda type thinking movie stars turned against the soldiers who were drafted in the Armed forces to fight and die in a Country that they were not supposed to win that war, they were there to die for a Country they did not want to fight for. Again, and again the powers that are, and now with the help of Obama and the Communist Democrats and Republicans will not allow our soldiers to fight the wars in Iraq and Afghanistan and win the way they were trained to win a war. Here again the Main Stream News Media is always demeaning our soldiers calling them murders and wanting them to go to trial for murder of civilians, who are the enemy and walk around in civilian clothes, our children walk around as live targets in their uniforms. The enemy knows who we are but we don't know who the enemy is.

To kill Americas youth, by our Government who legally send them to a war that is not for the freedom of that Country, nor is it to make them a Democracy it is called for by the UN, who is another enemy of the United States of America. When will the stupid Politicians we vote for see that we are being used by other Countries to kill our children so that they to will help Obama destroy the United states of America. The Middle-Eastern Countries are all Muslim and all Tribes and will always be Muslims first and are ruled by the Korean, religion, not by politics. The Muslims will never turn to a Democratic Government. Let the Muslims kill each other, it is not the job of the United States of America to help Country. If a Country attacks America like Saudi Arabia did when they flew the planes into the Twin Towers then we should attack them and wipe them out as they want to wipe us out now.

Every young man and women that Obama sends into harms way is one less person to make America strong, and that's his job. Weaken America by killing off as many people as he can and he is doing a good job. Every thing that Obama and his gang tell the American people is a lie. Obama wants to destroy the United States of America.

Government Health Care or Government Killer Care

The people of the Unite States don't want Government Health Care the President and the Marxist Democratic Congress and Senate do, and it's almost a sure thing with Al Franken in the Minnesota Senate seat. That's what we need another comedian in Government.

Why do the President and the Congress and Senate want Government Health Care? First let's look at the power they will have over life and death of the people, you can be sure that all the seniors, the Government will let die. Anyone with cancer young or old that is not connected to Obama's Marxist Government will die. Obama has no conscience, it does not bother him that he is responsible for the 50,000 or so abortion deaths that he and the Supreme Court made that the law of the land, and Obama giving millions of dollars to Foreign Countries to kill their babies, could we say that the Obama has made Judeo/Christian conspirators in mass genocide in the World. Obama doesn't care if 100,000 seniors or critically ill people die a month or year, he and the Marxist Democrats and Republican are stone killers. The people of the United States don't want this. Obama and the Marxist Democrats and Republicans want it. So how are Obama and the people we elected to represent what we tell them, what we want them to do, who they are supposed to work for us and do what we tell them?

Obama tells us it is for the poor, that is a lot of bunk; Obama's Health Care Plan won't help anyone. What ever the Government tells you is a lie, I have the Grand Avenue bridge for sale for a dollar, anyone want to buy that. That's what Obama's Health Care Plan is.

Obama and the State run news media are telling the people what a great thing that Obama wants to do. Go to any Country that has Government health care and they will tell you they can't even get to see a Doctor let alone get treatment for what ever is wrong with them. They are sent home to die. That means that a lot of seniors will die and people with serious illness like cancer will be sent home to die. How about a 100,000 people will die a year with the Obama Health Care Plan.

A lot of Marxist Countries don't mind this because they are for zero population, as is Prince Charles of England, whose new religion is earth first, people not at all. We must remember that all the people who are for Marxism are rich, Obama has not taxed them yet, and he will never tax them. Who are the rich in this Country that want Marxism, Obama and his family are so rich now that he sold out to everyone they will always get health care. The Marxist Congress and Senate made sure that they and their families will get real health care. The Congressmen and Senators also made sure that we the people will not get health care, you see we don't matter, the people that matter are in Obama's Gang, this way they can Rule the United States forever and their families must remain healthy so they can take their places when they die, with the help of ACRON and remain rich so they will stay in control for hundreds of years. That means all the Congressmen and Senators.

The Government says Medicaid and Medicare are broke and so is Social Security. The people didn't break any of these institutions, the Marxist Congress and Senate broke them with their big hearted give away programs with our tax dollars to any one who got to this Country legally or illegally they get all the benefits that belong to American Citizens who worked all their lives for Social Security they can't even get. A good example of Social Security give away, I had to go to SS board to fight for my SS, while I was refused my SS benefit there were six Muslims women who couldn't speak English at all were given SS benefits with no problem. No American Citizen can get what Foreigners can get. All the Congressmen and Senators are looking for are votes so they and their children can stay in Office and Rule the country. Look at the Kennedys, most of the Children are in the Congress along with Uncle Teddy. The Elite Politian's from the upper East Cost run the Government. There are so high class they are above even God. If you don't believe that, look them up on the internet.

So with Obama's Government Health Care Plan, what is the difference between the old time "Murder Incorporated" where people were murdered in cold blood for money and the Obama Health Care Plan where people will be murdered legally in the United States with the law on the Governments side. The people don't want Obama and his Marxist Government Health Care the Marxist Government does. Talk about a carbon foot print where everything that is touched is destroyed, the Congressmen and Senators and they have destroyed a lot of America and our freedom and they are going to wipe us out. From the very first conception of a Congress they never wanted an Army or a Navy that might take away the Congress's power to tax and control the people. Why do they want Citizens then?

This is a quote from John Adams, "Our founding fathers Representatives chosen for short term (no long term or for life) as should be render secure, the duty of expressing the will of their constituents (not their will, as we have now). What should we the people do, vote everyone out, no life time Congressmen or Senators limit their terms so they don't get to powerful to work against us and the USA. A few hundred years ago John Adams knew what he was talking about.

Never give up your right to own a gun. Guns are for freedom and Liberty, they stop Tyranny not voting. If Obama breaks the second Amendment which he is going to do in his second term, hide your gun never give them up go to jail if you have too, but don't give up your freedom. Obama's Gang Bangers will have their guns to keep the people in line; the thugs are coming with ACORN. Fight your Congressmen and Senators, e-mail them, phone them tell them what you want, if they don't do what you want make sure you tell them you are not going to vote for them and you will tell everyone you know not to vote for them

Government Subsidies or practicing Socialism 02/23/10

When did the Socialist/ Communist Democrats and Republicans start to subsidize every thing and every body in the United States of America? Could we say it started with Wilson and Colonel House who convinced Wilson and the Democrats and Republicans to create the Federal Reserve to handle the Treasury and making our money, which goes against the Constitution of the United States of American? And knowing human nature of people I am sure that all these Congressmen and Senators and we can't leave out the Supreme Court, whose job it is to follow the law of the Constitution and stop these fools from breaking it, did not stop them, so it stands to reason that Wilson and House offered all these people a huge money pay off that would last them and their families all their lives or until the Federal

Government took back the Treasury and the making of our money which they charge the tax payers millions of dollars in payment for this service. There are some theories that J.F.K. was murdered by the twelve banks of New York because he was going to stop the Federal Reserve from printing out money and put it back into the real Governments hands where it always belonged.

Could Government subsidize have started with Roosevelt when he incorporated Social Security? I did not realize that this was a form of Socialism, until I listened to Glenn Beck when he explained it, Beck is right, where the Government takes your money and puts it in the bank for you until you retire at 62 or 65, but the life expectancy in the thirties was 55 years old or somewhere in there, because those people from the 1920, 30 40 and even50's, as I remember them they all drank like pigs and smoked like chimneys. I remember going with my parents to visit relatives and the men would put a bottle of whisky in the middle of the table light up their cigarettes and didn't stop drinking until the bottle was gone, the women would go into another room by themselves and the children were put outside to play in the yard if there was one, if not you played in the street. None of these men reached the ripe old age of 65, they all started dying in there mid 40's. Could it have been that the Government was saving money for itself from our SS money to give it away to what ever or to whom ever, a Obama redistribution of the wealth way back then? But this was a good start for Socialism, and no one in the working class thought it was, they trusted the Government. We all thought that it was a nice thing that the Government was doing for us.

Now here comes Eisenhower, to get his roads built in the United States did he have to give up the SS money to the Congress and Senate to put it into a General Fund so they could steal it for themselves and give it away, which they started stealing it for themselves and their friends, in "Pork" as the term was used back then and "Ear Marks" which is used now, it sounds better, but it is still stealing on a big scale and giving the money away.

Then we come to the sixties and John F. Kennedy was elected President, the American people were very happy, we all loved J.F.K. he appeared to be like the regular people. During his short Presidency Hubert Hobart Humphrey the Senator from Minnesota, came up with a bill to help all the Black people in the United States to become first class citizens, who knew they weren't, also at this time Martin Luther King was marching all over the Country, but where ever he went there were riots in that city and the City burned. J.F.K made a speech where he said that he thought that it would be better for America if there was one big mix in our society to stop racism, racism will never stop, there is more racism in the Black community for themselves then there is in the white community. This bill Humphrey came up with was called Affirmative Action, where this socialist bill would prefer, and cause a real breach between the Black community and the White community, because if you were Black and didn't qualify for a job or a position you got the job and the white person did not. Then they extended this bill to include all women Black and White to be chosen over a White male. Now the Federal Government, Democrats and Republicans started subsidizing the Black Community with money, if a women wasn't married or the husband left, but he was still there in the background, all the women had to do is say her husband was gone and she the got money for every child she had. Mexicans and Puerto Ricans were put into this group. The Government, Democrats and Republicans went along and now the only real American was the American Indian, who migrated here during the Ice Age from Asia, China, Mongolia, and Siberia. So in reality they were the people here first but they were immigrants like the rest of the people in the world who came here, this is causing more racism. To this day all these people are being subsidized by the Federal Government and 85% of all Government jobs are held by the Black Community. A great Democratic voting base, I have heard some Black people scream that there wasn't enough Affirmative Action to satisfy them.

Jimmy Carter who created the trouble we now have in the Middle-East, and who keeps going to the Middle-East to talk to the enemies of our Country, really pulled off a the greatest Socialist money give away of all time with the help of Democrats and Republicans, that immigrants coming to this Country that are sixty-five or older collected over $2,000.00 a month from Social Security benefits, and he or she do not have to put one quarter of work to get all the benefits from it. Then Congressmen Dan Rostenkowski from Chicago a true Democrat got a law passed that if you had another pension, other then Social Security you do not get the money you are entitled too, even if you worked in the system all your life and were lucky enough to live that long. To this day if you are an American Citizen and you work all your life in the system you will not get the money you have coming if you have another pension plan.

Why are the illegal Mexicans and any other illegal who gets here by boat or plane and get lost in the country are able to get at least $1, 500.00 a month from Social Security per anchor baby, this includes the Muslims who in their religion can have four wives, we, the American tax payer and contributor to Social Security pay for all their children, they don't pay rent, they get free education and free health care. Why this can't be stopped, because the Socialist/Communist Democrats and Republicans and the State Run News- Media don't want it to stop. They are following the Cloward/ Piven strategy; overload the system and make it collapse and instill the new Communist Government. Even though our Communist President Obama and the hand picked Clinton administration want Socialist Health Care they are coming through the back door with the Cloward/ Piven strategy to kill the United States of America. If we survive this we must never trust the people we vote for to protect our rights and our freedom. Keep your guns keep buying ammunition because Obama, Holder, and the Socialist/ Communist, and John McCain do not want you to own a gun, McCain is a "One Eyed Jack" like Obama want you to think that he is a right guy working for American freedom, they are not.

The Socialist Democrats and bipartisan Republicans with out we the American people realizing it they have stopped all advancement of America into the 21st century and beyond, by subsidizing car companies, banks, you name it where they subsidized anything all forward movement to advance for the good of the people has stopped. Prices since the Socialist/ Communist Progressive Democrats and their allies the bipartisan Republicans have taken over, have tripled and taxes on every thing have tripled, look at your phone bill, look at any bill you have to pay and see what you are paying the Government in taxes. This a Carter left over from the Trilateral brain, Zbignew Brzezinski, an immigrant from Poland and an super intellectual Professor, are following the Carter Doctrine, raise taxes, double and triple what goods cost and you will lower the standard of living of all we American peasants to become Government slaves. Don't think so check it out.

Be ready for the rebellion. These people think that they are so powerful that they will destroy our God given rights to live in freedom. They think that because they control the armed forces and that Obama is creating a shadow Army and that the gang bangers and ACORN, the New Black Panthers and Muslims, who are training in this Country right now in urban warfare, will rise up and support Obama and the Socialist/ Communist Democrats and Republicans to stop us, why do you think that illegal Mexicans are allowed into this Country, why do you think that the Gangs are allowed to take over the cities and suburbs, why do you think that the Muslims are allowed one wife up front and three in the shadows, because Obama will use all these people to attack the people of the United States of America.

The Armed Forces should go with the people because they gave an oath to support the Constitution of the United States and not the Socialist/Communist Government created by the Democrats and Republicans that want to destroy the Constitution of the United States of America and the United States itself along with us. They did not swear to protect politicians; they swore to protect the American people from these Tyrants who are poised and ready to crush America.

May God help us in our effort to become a free people again and destroy the Socialist/Communist Democrats and Republicans who want to destroy us.

Hate crimes ready for a vote?

Congress has refused to define what a hate crime is. Are we to give up our rights to free speech all together because it will be called a "Hate Crime.?" No one can say they do not like someone because of his race, religion, or if they are Muslims or Homosexuals, we can no longer criticize President Obama or his staff, or the Politian's because we don't like the laws he is passing, that we might feel goes against we believe to be right. We cannot say that a man or women who committs a crime against a child are called pedophiles, we will be hauled off to jail and court to stand trial for some thing we said. I don't like such and such a movie will that be considered a hate crime?

I think that the Congressional Progressive Caucus, who take their orders from Institute for Policy Studies, who take their orders directly from Marxist Russia and Communist Party USA are trying to destroy the very thing that the Constitution of the United States based our freedoms on.

These 77 Congressmen are the most destructive Congressmen we have ever had. They control the Congress and the way the vote will go. They follow the Antonio Gramsci Marxist Manifesto on how to destroy the freedom of any Country and force it to become a Marxist State.

The bill that congress wants the Senate to pass now, 06/17/09 is completely vague there are no set rules or standards for what will be considered a hate crime. It could be any thing; a mother disciplines her child in front of anyone they can be arrested for a hate crime. If you use the "N" word will that be considered a hate crime, in other words you as a citizen of a freedom of speech Country will be silenced forever against saying anything. So now what, the 1600 witch hunts maybe even the inquisition could come back.

If bill S. 909 goes through look out, you work in a place and you might be in competition with a person who is a Homosexual, and he wants to knock you out of the competition all they have to do is call up the Government and say you said something bad about their Homosexuality. Bye, you're gone to jail and you said nothing against anyone. It could also be a person who is Black, Latino, or any other minority. All they have to do is say you said something against them. How about a pedophile has raped and murdered a child and you say something against him, someone calls up the Big Brother Government he goes free in the courts and you go to jail. And if you think that people are basically nice your wrong, people that I have seen all my life are small minded, selfish, egotistical, self-centered people looking to take advantage of any situation to get ahead and if this comes down, believe me people will use it against one another in a second. Also kiss the First Amendment good bye. Look out for the "do-gooders" they do more harm than anything on this earth

Government run Abortions

The true meaning behind Government run legalized abortions, which is legalized murder, by the Obama/ Pelosi/ Reid and Communist Democrats and Republicans which is only the beginning of the murder of all the people of the Unite States of America, it also has to do with zero population and the earth first group of nuts as a new religion and guess who is one the leaders of this Elite Group, the son of Queen Elizabeth, Prince Charles.

Today December 19th is a day of infamy with the caving in of democratic Senator Nelson from Nebraska for $400,000,000.00 on the Obama /Pelosi/ Reid Health Care Plan and Hilleary Clinton at the UN giving up our rights to keep and bare arms and with people like super intellectuals like John Holdren Obama's Science Czar this is what we have to look forward too. Now we must remember that Obama is here strictly to help the Communist Democrats and Republicans bring the United States to its knees and we will never recover. We must also remember that everyone in the Obama administration is from the Bill Clinton's Presidency, and John Holdren was his chief science man, now he is Obama's science czar, and the Clintons were in place to bring down the United States. They are both radical Marxist Elite thinkers.

Holdren's thinking is the same as Obama's and the Clinton's thinking that all women should be forced by law to have abortions, this is what Holdren wrote in his book in 1977 and his thoughts have not changed. Unfortunately the article I read about Holdren did not have an author's name to it and I am using this article to make my point. Holdren wants Compulsory abortions by law, under our existing Constitution, Single mothers should have their babies taken away by the government and they should be forced to have abortions. Mass sterilization of humans through drugs in the water supply as long as it doesn't harm livestock, it's OK to kill people but not OK to harm animals. Wasn't sterilization and a master race tried by Hitler and it didn't work. Are Obama/Pelosi/ Reid and the Communist Democrats and Republican now thinking that they are God?

The government could control women's reproduction by either sterilizing them or implanting mandatory long-term birth control devices in their bodies at puberty. This sounds like zero population guaranteed. The kind of people who cause "social deterioration' can be compelled not to have children...who will these people be? The Muslim are having babies eight to one over everyone in the United States and the Mexicans are second, does this mean that the Government controlled life and death over the people plan will stop these people from having children. I can see the white population and the black population under Holdren and Obama system of Communist Government being to forced to abort their children, because who will be the new slaves to Obama/ Pelosi/ Reid Communist Elite Rulers of the United States and the World. Holdren and Obama are thinking way ahead to a Planetary Regime and you thought that Obama was only thinking of the mother's right to have an abortion. All you have to do is change the parts of the Constitution, with the traitors that were helped to elect by Bush in 2006 I see these Communist Democrats and Republicans changing the Constitution to what ever they want. Isn't Obama getting people like Sotomayor put into the Supreme Court for just one reason to over throw the United States and make sure the Constitution is changed not for the good of the people but for the good of our new Rulers.

With Holdren's take on the Planetary Government will control everything in the World, you name it and the few super rich Elite people will control your very life, in each State and Country will have to have police power to enforce their thinking on you or you will have to be put to death if you don't fall into line, as Rahm Emanuel told Netanyahu because they are taking over the World

. That is Obama's and his man Holdern's thinking. Aren't Obama and Rahm Emanuel, doing just that with Obama's private "Green Army" training right now all over the United States is doing. Yet Janet Napolitano is naming, we the people terrorists, who have the nerve to say no to that great savior of the world and new Communist god Obama.

Holdren also says that this Planetary Government will have to loose its national sovereignty that this will insure that all natural resources will be controlled. The Communist Democrats and Republicans are doing just that by regulating the water ways and lakes in the United States right now. So this Obama/Pelosi / Reid Health Care Plan is more than reform health care it's about total control of our very lives. Why do you think Obama went to Copenhagen, to give up our sovereignty and why do you think that Hillary Clinton was at the UN giving up our second amendment rights to the UN. All of these things that all of Obama's administration is doing is to take away our freedom to destroy the Constitution of the United States of America and the United states itself.

When you see Obama on the TV soothing the people with his supposed calm trained voice and subliminal messaging we are lulled into a false sense of security that every thing will be alright. The dumbest statement I have ever heard in my life when John McCain said that if he lost the election for President that a Presidency under Obama wouldn't be bad, McCain knew that he was not supposed to be the President of the United States, he was chosen because he was the weakest candidate, he almost won because of Sara Palin, not because he was a great Statesmen which he is not. The United States of America is being choked to death by the Communist Democrats and Republicans and the only people to try and stop this destruction are the people who are the Tea Baggers, the rest of the United States cannot face our destruction and refuse to become part of the Tea Baggers trying to save the United States of America. They still refuse to believe that Obama is in control of what is happening to the America. This Obama/Pelosi/ Reid and Communist Democrats and Republican is not about health care it is about making us slaves to the Government. It is about legalized murder of ¾ of the population of America. It is about Holdren's Planetary Government. These are the kind of people Obama has surrounded himself with these are the people who are running the Country, and these are the kind of people that Obama is. None of these people believe in freedom or the United States of America they believe in the destruction of the United States of America.

Keep you guns handy and your powder dry. We will need them soon if we are to survive and live in peace and freedom.

Home grown terrorists in America

What is the difference between our home grown terrorists we have all over the United States than the terrorists in the Meddle-East? Our Government supports both. In the United States the Cities support them because they create jobs, since all the factories we had here are now overseas. We import about ninety seven percent of all the cars, dishes, medical drugs, and on and on and on. The gangs produce a lot of votes and a lot of money selling drugs, committing crime. It's puts a lot of judges, lawyers government police, F.B,I., etc, etc, to work.

Gangs terrorize the neighborhoods they control by terrorizing the people. Most people live in their homes behind half inch thick steel bars that include all doors and windows and some houses have ten foot high half inch bars around their yards to deter the gangs from barking into their homes. They use terror tactics to recruit new members as young as they can find. They intimidate them with beatings and threats of death, if they don't join the gang. Gangs have even recruited 10 years old to become assassins, why because they are children and cannot be tried for murder as an adult. They force young girls into gangs to use them as their prostitutes and put them into prostitution on the streets, using the same force. Where are the parents to stop this? Almost all the parents of today's gang members are or have been gang members all their lives. Where the humane public officials to protect these children from harm by are laws or by the police or the Politian's, so they have the right to live free and happy in their lives? Nowhere because they count on their votes to get them back into office. This is also slavery in the modern world you join the gang and do what the gang leaders tell you to do or you die a horrible death at their hands. Are they stopped by the local city and State or Federal Governments? No they are to busy forcing the legitimate none criminal people to give up `right to own a gun or rifle or anything else it takes to protect them selves from being murdered from any one group or religion, or Government, to life, liberty, and the pursuit of happiness. And what does our Liberal Socialist/Communist Democratic Government do to free these modern slaves? Nothing, they ignore what is going on. Because if and when the people rise up against the Government the gangs will be their police force as soon as the Liberal Socialist/Communist Democratic Government renders the free people of the United States helpless to defend themselves by taking away their right to own a gun to protect them selves from the terrorists that have grown up here in the United States for the last forty years.

With Obama, George Soros's million dollar contributor and anti gun leader, along with Nancy Pelosi, Harry Reid, and the liberal news media they will try with the UN to disarm the American Public so that the Gangs can help them rule while they are making history by destroying all the Freedoms of the United States and replacing it with Marxism.

Where is Janet Napolitano head of Home Land Security, another Bureaucrat and a Government Bureaucracy is a waste of tax payer's money that can only attack Veterans and Tea Party Citizens as would be Terrorists, but never go after the real terrorists, Gangs and Jihad Muslims that are training for Urban Warfare right now in Upper New York, and around the Country. Why won't the City, County, State, and Government do any thing to stop these Home Grown Terrorists, it is because that is what they want to happen. Between Obama's Marxist News Media and our Politian's they are lulling the public into believing we are safe and secure, far from it! We live in the most dangerous time in the History of our Country, Gangs and Muslim Jihadist, Castro, Chaves, Lulu from Brazil, China, Russia, North Korea, all of the Muslim World, are waiting for the word that America is now weak enough because of Obama and his Gang made America weak. The Gangs will be the first out of their neighborhoods to secure the streets and then the rest will come and Obama will be their leader.

If neighborhoods and Government Housing people live in terror it is because the parents allowed it to happen for money and power in their neighborhoods the police can't stop them or even slow them down, because of Political Corruption. By now in all the Cities across America Gang Bangers and Muslim Jihadist are being voted into City and State Governments and even into the Federal Government, they will control every thing. Look around. Bobby Rush, Black Panther leader, kill the Pigs and kill the white people. Obama's Marxist Government is out of control and the people have to take it back.

The only people that our Government has always wanted to enslave are the middle-class working man who are the strongest minded people in America and that is who they don't want to be able to defend themselves or own a weapon. Obama and his Marxist Regime are counting on the Gangs and Jihadist to help him take down America. Look at the tactics ACORN uses that are Obama's main Gang.

How to destroy the United States of America, the 100 year plan

All Countries and Civilizations though out history's leaders and Politian's have made plans for the future of their Countries to change them from what they were to what they want them to be, it all takes time. It doesn't matter that the planer of the take over or the wars it might take, will all have died, it only matters that the plan works and the new people follow the plan.

The Saudis under the leadership of King Abdulla have a plan that they are carrying out right now, when that plan was made had to be in his life time. The plan to take over the World by sending the Muslims into every Country in the World and populate it with Muslims, and they are doing it right now. All Muslims have four wives, in Countries like America where you can only have one wife by law, they still have four, and they are out producing the whole population of the United States 8 to 1. They will eventually take over the Government and will control all aspects of American Society and force everyone to submit to Islam or die. And they are willing to slaughter millions. The tax payers pay for all the children that the Muslim women have, like that the illegal Mexican babies anchor and subsidized Black communities and sect communities $1500.00 a month for each child.

The United States of America is now at the end of the 100 year old plan to destroy the Republic and the freedom of the America people. All the Progressive/Socialist/ Communist Democrats and Republican traitors are in place under the leadership of Barrack Hussein Obama, our closet Muslim President, Nancy Pelosi, Harry Reid to take over the World. To do this the have to destroy America, which they are happy doing, Obama and his Gang have taken over the General Motors, Banks and Obama has the nerve to tell Wall Street to work with him to destroy not only themselves but the whole Capitalist system, this guy thinks he can charm snakes out of tree, that he is earth's new god.

Who started the 100 year plan to destroy America and leave it for only the rich elites to live like the Royalty of the United States of America? Woodrow Wilson and his mentor Edward House,

who loved Socialism and Communism, he guided Wilson to incorporate, Racism, give to the twelve biggest banks in the Country to take over the printing of our money and pay them a huge fee for doing it. how could Wilson convince the Congress at this time in history to give away this, by making sure that they all, for the rest of their lives and their families lives forever as long as there is a Federal Reserve will receive money from this treasonous act against the American people. Wilson also started the UN, which at the time after WWI was called the League of Nations which didn't work then and is not working now. By the way Wilson was a big fan of H.G. Wells and he patterned the League of Nations after reading one of H.G. Wells dream book. Very smart for a super elitists and brilliant brain creating the first Illuminati, the take over of our money and the League of Nations which will and has been doing working against the United
   States of America.

Edward House also created The Council on Foreign Relations, not a Government agency but private that has always worked against the freedom of the United States of America, run by the wealthiest people in the world. David Rockefeller is the head of this organization, Rockefeller with the help of Zbigniew Brzezinski, called the Trilateral Commission who work against the citizens of the United States, where George W. Bush came up with the "New World Order" oppress freedom in the United States and turn America into a Communist satellite. Where only the rich are allowed to live like Kings and Queens of the World and the rest of us like slaves, strange that only the wealthiest people in America want this, and that includes the wealthy Progressive Democrats and Republican Congressmen and Senators including Barrack Hessian Obama. Almost every Congressman and Senator belong to the Council on Foreign Relations the Trilateral's and the Builderbergs also started by David Rockefeller.

How the Gulf States oil disaster may change.....

How the Gulf oil disaster may change the seafood culture of the Gulf States.

I read all three articles on this subject. Here is my take yes it will change the seafood culture of the Gulf States and put a ton of boats and people out of work.

A few weeks ago Obama wanted to regulate all fishing in the United States, no fishing in any of our rivers, lakes, and no fishing in the sea by anyone. So how convenient for the BP oil rig blow up in deep water and the Obama administration knew that it could not be fixed because of the depth, no diver could go that deep. There has been no fishing in the gulf for almost a hundred days and the oil is destroying the wetland sand the beaches and this is the season that the fishermen go out and harvest shrimp, and make some hard earned money. Obama and the second Clinton administration love disasters and because Obama wanted to stop all fishing and drilling off our coasts, could it be, that Obama and BP worked out a deal that they would have the oil well blown up. The Coast Guard allowed it to sink so that if there was an investigation there is no evidence left to check if it was a deliberate terrorist act to destroy the oil rig and stop the fishing in the gulf for Americans, and open the door for Russian and Chinese factory ships to come into our waters and fish them dry denying America Fishermen their right to make a living and denying the American people who make their living fishing work, and people fishing for pleasure, and we the people denied cost efficient sea food on our plates. This way Obama could make a great market for the Russians and Chinese to freely rape our coasts and charge the American people the highest prices that they could. Isn't this part of the Obama agenda to collapse another industry so the Government could take it over, more Government control more Socialism more people out of work, more of Cloward/Piven doctrine how to collapse the Country bring it to its knees and instill the Socialist thinking.

Then there is George Soros who controls most of Congress and the Presidency, to stop all drilling off our Coasts, didn't Obama give Brazil two billion dollars to start their deep, deep water drilling. George Soros would make billions and he would be happy to share that money with Obama and the Progressive Democrats and Republicans who work for him. Aren't there 80,000 jobs lost because of this oil spill, and again Obama wanted to stop all drilling off our coasts, so all the oil rigs would be moved to Brazil for the benefit of George Soros who is also working for the destruction of the United States.

Also isn't it strange that Obama never really talked to Governor Jendo of Louisiana, but always had other unknown people around him. Also didn't the Coast Guard pull in all the ships that were picking up the oil spills and stop them to check to see if they had enough life jackets, these orders don't just come from the Admiral they come from the President. Didn't Obama stop a ship that could pick up millions of gallons of oil in one day, didn't the people who run conservation stop all ships from scooping up the oil because they could only pick up 99% and not a hundred percent.

There is more to this oil spill than just the people in the Gulf States won't get their shrimp and other sea food. Look beyond Gulf Coast people not getting their sea food, in my opinion this oils spill was a deliberate act, to stop more people from making a living for them selves and getting more people dependent on Big Government.

Is Obama wasting our money ?

While Obama never personally gave a lot of money to Rev Wright's church, but when he became an Illinois Senator he funneled huge amounts of money to Reverend Wright's church. Obama gave Wright and Flagger hundreds of thousands of dollars of Illinois tax payers money thru grants, Obama also got Federal grant money funneled to Rev Wright, Father Flagger, and Louis Farrakhan, your money not his. Like he told O'Riely on his TV show, "I don't like writing checks out of my money, but he doesn't mind giving lots of money out of the tax payers' money. You can see how he spends tax payers' money now that he is President of the United States. Obama has parties every Wednesdays at tax payers' expense. These parties have the best of everything, food, liquor, music, he has the latest Rock bands and entertainers in the world and they get paid, by us, the taxpayers, it doesn't come out of his pocket. He doesn't mind spending our money while lavishly entertaining himself, and his friends there is more money where that came from, he thinks nothing of what the coasts the tax payers, just pay it. I wonder how much money he funneled to Rev. Wright, Fr. Flagger, and Farrakhan with the stimulus package.

Obama and his wife love parties, they are party people, they attended very party that was given, by the Elite people of Chicago, when he was a Illinois Senator. Then he tells the United States we are going to have to suffer, in the summer don't turn the thermostat lower you might be wasting energy, in the winter you will have to be a little colder. Obama and friends don't have to suffer they are now the Ruling Elite Class of the United States of America and we are the Government slaves. He and the Marxist Democratic Party are going to save the world by going Green, that is a lot of bunk. All Obama wants to do is to make the working man's standard of living go lower than what it is now. Obama and the Marxist Democrats are going to raise the gas price up to the magic number of $4.00 a gallon to force us to buy cars that we don't want and are too small, and you still won't get the gas mileage you want. He is not doing it to clean the air, as the Green leader Al Gore says, Obama has an obligation to Detroit to get rid of these pieces of junk that they manufactured because of the Marxist Democrats told Detroit to do and the people won't buy as long as the gas is below $4.00 a gallon. I wonder how much of a commission he will get from the car manufactures for their part in robbing the people of free choice. If Detroit wanted to make money, and I have said this before, all they have to do is put out a large comfortable car powered by a V8 that can give you over 50 MPG into the Car Dealers lot and they will sell overnight. They can do it but, I don't know when the American public will wake up and know that every thing that the Democrats do is to kill progress of America moving forward, the car companies can do any thing they want. But as long as they take money from the Federal Government they will be and are run by, and this is a good example of Socialism/ Marxism of the Government running things we the People are out of luck. We are going to get what the Government wants' us to have not what we want to have.

If any one is interested in what Obama distribution of wealth is, watch the movie Dr. Zhivago when he comes back from the War there are five families living in his house. That is pure Communism, that's redistribution of wealth. The poor move into your house and you move out and are placed in a Government Project House or in another Country by law, just as Obama has legalized the murder of new born babies. Obama and his followers will live in mansions while the rest of us will live, if we are allowed to live, live in garbage. This way the Marxists Democrats will "level the playing field" and they will show the world that they have at have broken the back of Freedom, Life,

Liberty, and the pursuit of Happiness of America. They, the Marxist/ Socialist Democrats will still have all the money and we will have none. The Marxists Democrats and Republicans will never loose an election because Obama's Army of ACORN will see to it that there will never be an honest election in the United States of America. He gave millions of our tax dollars to ACORN so they can steal the votes for Obama. Just as they did for his Presidential election and as they did in Minnesota no will dare stop them, because ACORN will play the race card, and we paid for this through our tax dollars that Obama gave to ACRON. We basically paid to destroy free elections.

Obama has no concept that every time he takes Air force One any where in the world he costs the tax payers millions upon millions of dollars. He doesn't take only one huge airplane he has to take at least three or four, because he and his entourage of people, cooks, Treasury Agents, guests, news people, cars, cooks, doctors and Military personal cost the tax payers millions of dollars, he does not mind it doesn't come out of his pocket. If his travels did any good that would be fine, but they don't he is not a Statesmen he will always be a street organizer working for ACORN. Yet to him and the rest of the Marxist Democrats and News Media we the people have to suffer and become poor to satisfy the world. Wake Up America you have been taken for a ride.

Jimmy Carter the Trilateral Commission destruction of America

It is hard to believe that Democratic and Republican Senators and Congressmen and Presidents from Jimmy Carter's reign, except for Ronald Regan, have followed the Carter doctrine of the destruction of the United States of America. Raise our taxes and lower our standard of living to make all of Europe happy, most of all Germany. Follow the Trilateral Commission's Doctrine of destroying America. Sell out to the enemy where ever and when ever you can. Make people ashamed of being an American, split the Country in two with Multiculturalism and two languages, have no loyalty to the United States Constitution, Bill of Rights, or to our selves. To follow England in becoming

Politically Correct to help the demise of America to be lead by European laws and thinking, every one who has ancestors who came to the United States ran from the oppression of European elites and their Governments to live here and be proud of be- coming a United States citizens and be free to raise their families and practice the Religion they believe in to become rich if they were smart enough, the only people, the Muslims who come to the United States not to be free to practice their Religion and , not to become Americans but to overthrow the people of the United States and force us to bow to their Religion, to believe in there moon god, and live in a Country, like our new Obama/Pelosi/ Reid Communist Government wants to turn the United States into. We have been sold out of our Rights as Free People; we are going into Slavery to the Obama oppressive Communist Government Doctrine. Obama and his Communist Government are breaking the laws of our Country the Constitution of the United States of America, and not a single Congressmen or Senator is stopping them from destroying the Constitution. Not even that great liberal idealist on the Supreme Court who are supposed to know the law of the land and like our elected officials protect our Constitution and feedom.

All of these Communist Congressmen and Senators for over thirty years have been pushing the Carter/ Zbigniew Brzezinski, a Polish emigrant was to Carter as Edward House was to Wilson, where all the trouble we have today started. The Trilateral Commission, the Council on Foreign Relations, Bilderbergs and European Nations all working for a one Elite super rich class run to the World. They are the super Elite who come out of the East Coast, and the Elite Eastern Establishment, the Federal Reserve Bank of New York, 12 Banks, who are not owned by the Government but by the ruling class of the East coast, the Rockefellers, the Bush's, the Kennedy's and at the low end the Kerry's just to name a few, Chase Manhattan, Citibank, Morgan Guaranty Trust, Chemical Bank, Manufactures Hanover Trust, is this a German Bank? Bankers Trust Company, National Bank of North America, Bank of New York, basically the Federal Reserve Bank is and has been owned by the wealthiest Elite from President Wilson's time the Rockefellers, J.P. Morgan, their families still own the Federal Reserve Banks of New York. There is also a rumor that the Rothschild World Bank also owns a big share of the Federal Reserve Bank. The point being that the East coast Elite's run the Government. And they all went to the Elite Colleges on the East Coast, Harvard, Princeton, Yale, Dartmouth and other college's at a minimum of $45,000.00 a year not including room and board, and other colleges through out the United States where young people who have no knowledge of what it takes to make a living are brain washed not to use their new found smart brains to work toward the good for themselves and the United States of America. They are taught to hate America and all that we stand for and if they become part of the Trilateral Elite Commission or get a place in the "Communist Think Tanks or they should become elected to the Congress or the Senate or even into City and State Government they are taught to be disloyal to America, rob America, sell America out to our enemy's rob and cheat the people and to legally murder millions of Americans a month through the Obama/Pelosi/Reid Health Care, and to help destroy America so that they will rule the World. That is what Jimmy Carter thinks he is a ruler of the World and that is what our Congressmen and Senators think they are.

All the Congressmen and Senators think they will be the Rulers of the World, all the wealthy Élites think the same. There is only one obstacle that is standing in their way and it's the United States of America and the Constitution and the Bill of Rights, and our God given rights to live as free people. Not as slaves to the Trilateral Commission, The Builderbergs, or to the Council on Foreign Relations or the abstract thinkers like Brzezinski, and Kissinger, just to name a few. Brzezinski one of the founders of the Trilateral Commission was the real President with Carter, or the Rockefellers, the Bush family the Kerrys, the Kennedys, the Pelosi's, Frank, Dodd and now the real Ruler and God of the World Barrack Hussein Obama, the coldest blooded killer in the history of mankind. Treason means nothing to these people because they control the Government.

America is ready die, being bled to death by these people for years that I have written about, some people cry out for truth, but they do not tell all the truth. Are they part of the plan just to give, we the people lip service where we might have a little hope that our world and country will be saved by some miracle? Or should we, the real lovers of freedom and America rise up and crush our oppressors before they can crush us. Keep your guns well oiled and keep you bullets dry, we will need them soon.

If we beat these people in the 2010 elections they should have term limits, Senators should never serve six years they should not get better than we the people, they should serve 2 years and not be able to run more than twice and that goes for the Congress, and the President. The President should not have the power he has today. And there should be no lobbyists at all, and the Federal Bureaucracies should be cut back to the bare bones the same way they cut back on us. A good example of a bureaucracy that should be dumped all together is the Department of Energy in forty they were supposed to find alternative energy to keep us out of becoming dependent on foreign oil. It costs the American public $45, 000, 000, 000 .00

a year to keep this monster bureaucracy running, they cannot even find an alternative rest room, they have done nothing to help this Country in all existence but suck up tax payers dollars and pension funds for nothing.

If the Jimmy Carters and the Communist Democrats and Republicans would have kept their noises out of the private sector and the car companies weren't so greedy for Government money they would have found the alternative to foreign oil consumption, so all the Federal Government does is give lip service to the people and nothing gets done for we the people but everything goes to Foreign Countries so they can turn around and use our money they make from us to destroy America.

By now, if the Federal Government wasn't in the mix, we could have every American made car powered by a atomic energy chip no bigger than a silver dollar powering our cars at five hundred horse power for five hundred years and the middle-east would have gone back to camel herding instead of wanting to buying and buildings arms of mass destruction to help our President and the Communist Democrats and Republicans ready to destroy the United States of America. We could really be living better than any country in the world where there would be no killing deceases, no corruption, and a Communist Government that finds that we the America people are their enemies.

John McCain is a super Progressive Bipartisan Socialist

John McCain is no better then his President Barrack Hussein Obama when it comes to Government take over of every part of freedom loving Americans. While going through my e-mail I read an article that said that John McCain reaching across the aisle and his new party the Bipartisan Party wants a bill passed that will give the FDA, the power to regulate over the counter drugs, vitamins food supplements and everything else he can think of for the Government to regulate. This will work directly against we the people, in higher prices, and free choice of what we want to do with our lives to be more healthy, not what McCain wants. Who are these Progressive Politicians who think that they are and they alone should and can tell the people what we can and cannot do and what we eat and drink, think or chose to do in our daily lives or anything else that we want to do. They are the Parents of all the people. So where is McCain any better then Obama?

When he was running for President he said, "It won't be bad if Obama is elected President"

McCain has worked with every Progressive Liberal Socialist/Communist Democratic and Republican Senator there is. He voted along with Hillary Clinton and other Socialist/Communist Democrats and Republicans to make the United States a two language Country, he voted yes to take away our right to own a gun of any kind, he voted for multiculturalism, where no one is an America even if you were born here. All these Progressive Socialist/ Communist voting go against us the American citizen. McCain will vote for Obama Government Health Care. McCain has voted for amnesty for all illegal Mexicans, he voted for them so they can get a driver's license, money from Social Security, rob the American people of their tax dollars and their Social Security pensions. An illegal Mexican can walk into any State driver's license office and get a driver's license with out any ID all he or she has to say is that they are illegal aliens with no fear of deportation. With of Progressive Socialist/ Communist Democrats and Republicans wanting to over throw and destroy the United States of America, they have also made it OK for illegal Mexicans to vote in all the coming elections in every State that have infiltrated that is why Obama and all the

Communist Democrats and Republicans can do and are doing their undermine of our freedom. If any one reads this they better call their State legislators and stop this illegal voting by the "new voters block that Obama and the Progressive Socialist/Communist Democrats and Republicans are doing to us. When Obama says, with a grin on his face that he is not a Socialist, like Nixon said he was not thief, Obama is worse, he is a true hard core Communist.

During the election Presidential campaign John McCain was loosing big time in the polls, all of a sudden McCain comes up with millions of dollars to finance him. What happened? McCain was more unpopular than any of the other candidates and he was chosen to loose and make it easier for Obama to win. McCain never attacked Obama on his Liberal stance of Big Government or any other thing that the Progressive Socialist/Communist Democrats wanted. The polls showed that Obama was going to win, and to make sure that McCain would loose he came up with and duped Sarah Pallin to run as his choice as Vice President, knowing that there has never been a women elected with the running mate for President! All of a sudden his campaign took off because of Sarah Pallin, if she was running for President at that time she would have won. McCain did everything in his power to loose the election.

When he lost and McCain made sure that he would loose to Obama he ripped Pallin apart blaming her for his failure to win the Presidency and now a a year later Pallin is indorsing McCain to run as Senator after what McCain did to smear her. Then she is a Progressive Socialist/Communist Republican that should not be elected to any office. This east cost and movie garbage that when you stick it to some one it's not personal its business that's a lot of hog wash, you stick it to a person and try to destroy their reputation their honesty or integrity or make them look like a fool, that is personal, there is no such thing as it's only business. Watching the put up job yesterday on TV with Obama pushing his Health care and his take over of the freedom of the people of the United States and the Senators and Congressmen all sitting there listening to him as if he were some thing special and McCain took a back seat to Obama again, when Obama told him they were not on the Campaign trail, that was over, he won, and McCain wimped out and sat down like a good little boy, what does that tell you about McCain. He may be a Viet Nam hero for what he did, but he is not for American freedom or the Bill of Rights or the Constitution McCain is for the Progressive Socialist/ Communist Democrats and Republicans big government. What Obama did to McCain was personal. And he sat down like a good little Progressive Obama person. At the end of this phony meeting every one of the Republicans walked up to their leader, Obama, patted him on the back shook his hand and apologized to him for not going along with him. That tells me that there is no difference between Republicans and Democrats they are all Progressive/Bipartisan Socialist, Communist ready to take away our freedom. Except for a few Republicans who have the guts to not go along with Obama's Communist take over of health care and the legalizing of the murder of senior citizen first and people over 55, why do you think Obama wants to lower the age to collect a pension The only real thing that has happened is that we the People got to-gather it is because we the People have risen up to fight the Government tooth and nail to stop Obama and all Progressive Socialist/ Communist Democrats and Republicans from taking over our lives.

It is not the dumb young people, who think because they are educated in the College's of hate and their Progressive Socialist parents like John McCain's daughter and his wife's thinking. It is the everyday working man and women and every senior citizen who has been educated and come up from the school of hard knocks that have stopped the Progressive Obama Socialist/ Communist Communist Democrats and Republicans from destroying our Country. When Obama says he is not a Socialist he is right, Obama is more

than that he is a true Communist, look at his back
ground and look who he has surrounded himself
with, look who raised him look at who his mentor
was look at his education ALL COMMUNISTS.

Marxist Democrats and Republicans attack the honest citizens

Again and again the Marxist Democrats and Republicans attack the honest citizens of America. Obama is using his Clinton appointees to take away our freedoms while staying in the back ground because if anyone points a finger at him he will claim his innocents, " I didn't do it, they did it." So he will be innocent of all blame when he and he alone is the person who gives the commands for his gang to do his bidding. This way he won't loose any votes. Yet in the mean time we will have no freedom or liberty, Obama will have exactly what he wants, Marxism and slavery of the people.

Everyone in his cabinet wants to destroy the Second Amendment, no guns for the normal citizens of America the Congressional Progressive

Caucus who want to destroy the United States of America. Now Obama has czar who wants the hunting of animals stopped, and says that each animal should have a lawyer to defend its rights. That's one reason the new czar wants to take away hunting rifles. Where did Obama find these people? Why are the Congressmen and Senators so afraid of the American Citizen owning a gun or any other weapon if they want to own one or a dozen and the ammunition to go with the weapon? They say because people will die. I don't see the honest, God fearing America citizen going around killing people. But I do see our own home grown terrorist, the gang bangers taking over Cities and towns all over the United States. I see gangs murdering people every day for no reason except the control of dope, Chicago Illinois gang banger heaven, New York, gang banger haven, Los Angelis, even in Alaska, the Mexicans gangs taking over the South West. I don't see Obama and his Gang trying to outlaw the Gangs. I don't see Eric Holder or Hilary Clinton, Brady, Bidden, or any other Congressmen or Senator trying to outlaw the Gangs and getting their weapons. They want ours! Obama doesn't want the Gangs touched because he is for the Gangs that's is one of the things he voted for when he was a senator in the Illinois Government, why because he could count on the Gangs and Acorn to twist arms and break heads if the people didn't vote for Obama. The whole of the Obama Organized Crime Marxist Government want to destroy the American people. He can double talk all he wants and the State Run news media can lie about how high his numbers of approval are high, I wouldn't believe the State run news media if they swore on a stack of bibles let alone the Obama and his Marxists Government.

Ask yourself why the parents allow their children to be recruited into the gangs, the boys go in to become murders, thieves and drug dealers, and the gangs force the girls to become prostitutes for the gangs and on the street. The reason the parents allow all this to happen is the money they get from their children, the parents don't care about their children they care about the dope money. Where is Obama, Feinstein, Boxer, Pelosi, Clinton and all the rest of the Marxist Government trying to take away the gang bangers guns and power they have. You put the gang bangers in jail they live a good life they still have the same freedom they have on the streets the only thing they don't go home at night. They have money, dope, and sex, with men or women. They run the prisons the way they want. The gangs in America are so powerful they defy the law of the land and get away with it because of the ACLU, National Lawyers who Hillary Clinton made sure she funneled money to them, Guild, Center for Constitutional Rights, plus the Marxist Government and the State run news media, to defend them. And the State run news media to make excuses for them. All the above are and were communist run organizations to destroy the United States.

Obama and his gang want chaos in the United States, keep the people off balance do what ever Obama can not to let the people unite feed them disinformation and propaganda never tell the truth. Why don't Obama's new media tell the people how bad law and order have broken down in the Gang controlled Cities and towns? The gang bangers get away with everything they do. Where do the Obama Marxist Government and the Obama news media put the blame? They put the blame on honest people it is our fault because we want to hang on to our second amendment rights that say we have the right to protect our lives and our families' lives and our property. Obama's disinformation tells us the Mexican Gangs get their weapons from us the people we sell them the weapons to kill us with. Why doesn't the Obama news media tell the truth where the Mexican gangs get their weapons, they get their weapons from Cuba and his friend Chaves who get the weapons from China, and sell them or give them to the Mexican Gangs. Not from America.

The reason Obama Clinton, Feinstein, Boxer, Pelosi, the 77 Congressional Progressive Caucus protect the gangs is that the Gangs will be their Army to control the people when Obama Marxist take over the United States of America. As soon as Obama gets through bankrupting the United States and bankrupting the Banks the United States of America will be sold to any foreign Country that has the money. Where will all the Marxist Democrats and Republicans be? They are now rich beyond their wildest dreams because they stole every dime out of the treasury, and they will be safe from poverty. George Soros has his bid in to buy America with the help of Obama and senators like Schumer and other traitors that we have elected to keep America free and safe.

Stand up to the Obama Marxist Government. Don't let the Congress and Senators destroy our wealth and freedom. We are millions they are a few

Mary Landrieu senator form Louisiana

Senator Mary Landrieu got $300,000,000.00 for her vote on Obama, Pelosi, Reid Communist Health Care Plan, that will kill not only 50 to 60 thousand senior citizen a month it also kill every terminally ill child at about the same rate as senior citizens, and all the women and men with cancer and other costly deceases. Mary Landrieu who comes from a long line of political family that ran the State of Louisiana and taught her well about corruption and taking money she sold out every citizen in the United States of America. Reid knew she was salivating for money and he gave her $300,000,000.00, not Reid's money but our money, the tax payers. If Reid and Pelosi and Obama can give millions and billions of dollars away to there constituents and any organization who sticks their hand out and give themselves raises, and raise their expense money in millions and pay for all their trips and they all go first class with family and friends why should we have to pay more and more taxes we the people don't benefit from our own tax money they just bleed us to death. If we don't pay our taxes the IRS, the Gestapo of the United States, will take everything you own and leave you in the street, unless you are an illegal Mexican or other illegal coming into this Country sucking the American citizen's tax money dry, or if you are a Congressman or Senator you are exempt from paying income tax, the Obama, Pelosi, Reid and every Communist Democrat and Republican allow them to get free health care, free education, and housing, they don't have to worry about being in this Country illegally they get a free pass. The American Citizen doesn't, that shows that the every President and the Communist Democrats and Republicans do not respect we American Citizens, they are really against us. Try and go to another Country as an illegal immigrant, including Mexico, they will throw you in jail where you can rot with out a trial or a free lawyer and none of their laws that pertain to their citizens.

The Communist Democrats and Republicans, Senators and Congressmen that voted to pass Obama/Clinton Health Care will never give the people of the United States Health Care, no one will get Health Care, the Congress and Senate have just sentence everyone of to death before our time. That means you and your family. They robbed the Treasury and kept most of the money for themselves, they are very free living with our tax dollars, and they want to kill us, they don't even have to put death camps they have something better than that, a Death Panel, just like they have in all the Socialist/Communist Countries in the World. We the United States of America were the only really free people of the World, now that the Communist Democrats have leveled the playing field we will be like the rest of the World, all the Citizens will be poor and will be put to death by our own Government, I hope that every person who voted for Obama and lost their business and jobs are happy because now they are going to lose their lives, by the law of the land that a small minority of people we elected to keep us free and strong and wealthy have just voted to destroy us.

Well if they the Obama-Pelosi-Reid Senators and Communist Congressmen have voted that we the people should die because we are sick and need medical care now not ten years from now or having to have our lives decided by a death panel, and includes our children, shouldn't we the real American people stand up for our lives and take their lives and their families lives, as they are making it a law that the Obama Communist Government want to take our lives from us. Isn't it a God given right that you should live and not die because of Obama's Communist Government or are we stupid cattle being lead to the slaughter happy to die for Obama-Pelosi-Reid and all the Communist Democrats and Republicans in Washington. They don't have to die or become poor just us.

They are nothing; they think that the Armed forces will protect them against us. I don't think so; the Armed Forces have sworn to uphold the Freedom of the people of the United States from a Tyrant Government and any enemy of this Country we have them here and now. The Armed Forces do not take an oath to protect the President, his staff, or Congressmen and Senators, they have sworn to uphold the Constitution of the United States of America and Obama- Pelosi- Reid and the Communist Congressmen and Senators have all gone against the Constitution and the Bill of Rights and the people of this Country and they have also gone against our Armed Forces by not giving them the money they need to fight and protect themselves, by sending them like prostitutes to fight for other Countries and when they get there to give up their lives, the Government ties their hands behind their backs so they cannot even protect themselves from the brutal people they are fighting.

These Communist Democrats and Senators don't want to give our soldiers, sailors and airmen the health care they need after they have been mangled and mutilated by War. Obama wanted them to pay for their own wounds, quote from Obama, "You are all volunteers no one asked you to join the Armed Forces," Obama even wanted the Armed Forces to Pledge their allegiance to him and not the Country or the people. We the people have to fight back harder against these oppressors of our freedom than all the Wars that have been fought around the World. Keep your guns, keep your faith in God as Obama told the World that we are a bunch of a———-s who believe in our guns and God. If we have to have a Rebellion...so be it. I will give up my life for the Freedom of my United States of America.

Our Armed Forces will also suffer death from this Health Care Plan, let one of them develop cancer or get wounded where they have no arms or legs what good would it be to save these Soldiers, Sailors, Marines, they will not be able to serve Obama-Pelosi- Reid's Communist Democrats and Republicans, they will be given a lethal injection to die because it is cheaper then taking care of them. If you think that these Communist Democrats and Republicans won't do this think again, if they are will to kill millions of unborn babies here in the United States, and now the people they are ready to wipe us all out for Obama and his Communist Government they will always be able to start all over again. They have the so called poor and the illegal Mexicans to work for them.

Why then if Obama doesn't want to kill all the Citizens of America, why does he want to save the Gitmo Terrorists if he were not a closet Muslim, he said in his book he is for the Muslims. Obama ordered it and Holder carried it out. Obama already has set them free by telling everyone in the World that were tortured by us. The ACLU is jumping for joy, and Holder's law firm has defended all of them for year's, pro-bono. And the Obama-Pelosi-Reid Communist Government wants to kill the American people and our troops. See if anyone can get a fare trial in any Muslim Country. They would cut you to pieces slowly just to enjoy seeing you suffer. The Health Care is just one more way the Obama-Clinton-Pelosi-Reid Communist Democrats and Republicans can kill us all.

Medicare, Medicaid, and who are the poor in America?

While watching a mainstream news media TV station this morning 08/12/09 a real staged and set up of a couple thousand people waiting outside, the news commentator said they have been waiting outside this Clinic in Los Angelis California all night for medical treatment. And who were these people, they were all Black and illegal Mexicans who claim they don't have health insurance. But they were all dressed very nice some in the latest fashions and all had cell-phones. 90% of these people were at this Clinic to get their teeth fixed free and eye glasses for free. The news commentator is a real actor his face was sad for these poor people, it made me sad to think that the main stream news media is still pushing Obama death care medical program.

There are no destitute poor people in the United States of America it is a lie and propaganda put up by the Marxist Obama Government with the help of the mainstream news media pushing Obama's socialized medicine. First of all the poor people on welfare are doing ten times better than the people that have to work for a living. They get free housing, free education, free money, they get free health care, they drive around in BMW, Mercedes, new Chryslers, they are all fat from the food they eat. They all have 50" plasma TV hanging on their wall in the apartments they live in. A few weeks ago the news paper ran a story about Black women who has lived in the welfare system all her life, the Government takes care of the poor quite well she has a 50" plasma hanging on her wall and she is complaining that the Government isn't doing enough for her. The poor welfare people all have a street scam going where they can make money on the side, income tax free, that is how they can own BMW's Mercedes and other top shelf cars. If the welfare people are sick or ragged looking it is because of drug abuse and alcohol. If they have no hope that is because the Federal Government destroyed any ambition that these people would have because they are raised to just keep your hand out you don't have to anything. That is Socialism at work. Kill any ambition that people have in their make up. These people are the so called poor by choice with the help of the Federal Government. Yet all these poor people have money to throw away on booze and dope.

The Government and AARP have made statements that their 45,000,000 poor and uninsured people that are starving in the United States of America. The numbers are lies put up by the ARRP, Obama and the Marxist Congressmen and Senators, the main stream news media. There may be say a couple million people that live under bridges and in allies in card board boxes, but those are the people that were turned out of all the State run mental intuitions in the United States because it was costing the States to much money to take care of these people, men and women so they turned them out into the streets. These people need help but they don't know it because they are mental. That was a very cruel thing that the States did to save money. The main stream news media didn't say a word. What did the States do with the money that was allocated to take care of the mental institutions?

Obama clams that he wants his killer Medicare right now to help the poor. The poor or welfare people get every thing they want. They already get free medical care it's called Medicaid and they can also get SSI, for their children, more money, just slap the child in the head a few times before they take them in to make the SSI board think that the child has some thing wrong with it and they get more money from Government run Social Security.

There are no starving poor adults, children or seniors as AARP has eluded too. There are so many State run free meals, street organizations that will feed the people. Free lunch at all the schools for the poor children, no child will go hungry. No senior will go hungry because of meals on wheels, and they all get Medicaid. The best is even the illegal Mexicans and other illegal people get free medical attention, free housing, free education and college students get free housing. This is a great one, Jimmy Carter thought this one up and the Congress passed this into law to drain more from the working tax paying people, this has been going on for 30 years or more. An legal or illegal alien who comes into the United States who is sixty five or older will receive a Social Security pension of a minimum of $2,000.00 a month, no wonder every body wants to come to America, it's great the stupid Americans give them all the free money they gave and free medical, free everything, but if you are 65 and want to collect your Social Security pension that you worked 120 credits and all your life for you will be lucky to a $1,000.00 a month. Now the Muslims are here and there are other sects that have more then one wife and each wife has many children they get money from Social Security and they don't have to contribute.

Guaranteed that the Muslims all have 4 wives as the Koran tells them, but because polygamy is against the law they don't declare them as wives and the Government doesn't check up on them.

The reason Medicare, Medicaid, Social Security are going broke and Obama, Nancy Pelosi and the Marxist Democrats and Republicans want to start killing off Senior Citizens and anyone who has a life threatening decease no matter what age as soon as possible is to reduce spending. Yet in Obama's Medicare package he is allowing millions upon millions of dollars to make walking paths, bike trails and more basket ball courts where people can go and become healthy or get mugged by the gang bangers and our teen agers can get recruited into the gangs. That is the demented mind Obama and his gang have.

I saw a chart that was on TV last night and it was a scale of life and death, made up by Dr. Death himself, Emanuel. Life to him and the rest of the insane Government is that the only people worth saving are 10 year olds to 35 year olds the res cost to much money to be considered, that means that the real thinking of how to kill more United States Citizens is that anyone over thirty five is not worth the Medical expense and should die. And Obama and Nancy Pelosi and the Marxist Democrats and Republicans are serious and they tell us this with a straight face, like you don't understand this? But this is not for them they are the "Great Ones" and Obama is their new God, and we the people are nothing. Life is becoming very cheap in the United States, when our leaders look at the people and say you die. Every word that comes out of Obama's mouth about his Medicare plan is a lie, his town hall meetings are a set up, his news conferences are a set up. Do you or do we want to die because we can't get medical treatment. No! Obama wants us to die; Obama wants to kill the United States of America with the help of Nancy Pelosi and the Marxist Democrats and Republicans. They lie and Obama lies, Obama thinks he can charm a snake out of a tree, and Obama thinks that we the people are stupid and will say OK I'll let you kill me with your new Health Care Plan. We the people are not stupid. Be careful Obama where you think you and the rest of your world wide Marxist friends think you and Nancy Pelosi and the Marxist Democrats and Republicans can take us. I refuse to look to Obama as a President or leader of the United States of America. Obama hates America, he hates white people, he hates the Jews, he hates our freedom, and he is a stone killer of mankind. Obama was and is a trained Communist form his child hood, and his job is to destroy American freedoms and kill all the Americans he can. We can no longer trust the Congressmen and Senators, even in our State, County, and City Governments, we can no longer trust the mainstream news media. Boycott all the liberal movie stars movies. Boycott all liberal news papers, get rid of all the teachers who teach our children to hate America, don't let Obama take our beliefs in Jesus Christ as our Christen God. The people that Obama really cares about are all the Marxist Countries in the World and the Muslims, from his own words and form one of his books, "If push comes to shove I am for the Muslims"

Moving America into Marxist/ Socialism

Does any one remember Nikita Khrushchev in September 1960 at the UN beating his shoe on the desk in front of him yelling "We will bury you..." slowly but surely Communism/Marxism has crept into the United States of America, education in our Colleges to brain wash the inexperienced young adults who know little of the real world outside their homes, where they were protected from the ugliness of the world. Marxism has infiltrated into our society through every under handed way they could. Through the Marxist news media through think tanks through the ACLU. We saw Marxism really come alive in the Sixties during the Viet Nam War. Marxism has gained strength that is unbelievable to this current day. We are ready to be buried.

The grave digger is here. He is Barrack Hussein Obama. How is Obama going to get the United States into Marxist Socialism? Do you think after his conversion of America to Marxist/Socialism and he and the Marxists Democrats will have a great purge of the people who were against him and charge them with a crime and send them to jail where they will mysteriously die. Purge all who do not except him as the Ruler of the United States of America. Like they do in Russia.

After Obama's mother left him in Hawaii with her parents, his Communist/ Marxist education began. From his early childhood by his grandfather first and then introducing him to his best friend Frank Marshall Davis, Communist/ Marxist oriented writer, to take Obama under his wing and brain wash him through his early childhood and into adolescence into the Communist/ Marxist ultra thinker he is today. If not why would he run to the Occidental College that further completed his education in hate America and change it to Marxist/ Socialism? Occidental College is linked to the Communist Party USA, which Frank Marshall Davis is linked to. After two years he left Occidental College and went to Colombia University. Did he major in Antonio Gramsci's Marxism while he was there, then on to Harvard to study law and more Marxism? Who paid for all of his education?

Obama after arriving in Chicago found another Communist/Marxist American terrorist Bill Ayers who he became friends with. Sitting in Bill Ayers home and listening this mentor convincing him more and more that the United States should become a Marxist Country and how it should be done after he captured the Presidency, and Obama knew he was to be President long before anyone ever heard of him because he was trained as the Manchurian Candidate from the time he was a boy. He was chosen by the powers that want to wreck this Country and given great marks by the Professors who are connected to Russia and the elite of the World. That's why on TV he acted like he was the President even before the Election. He was the President. He cleared the whole field of all the candidates.

Obama has surrounded himself with Communist/ Marxist people his campaign manager, David Axelrod, a Marxist thinking person with a great deal of sponsorship and knowing where to get all the money Obama needed to get elected President. Rohm Emanuel, Communist/ Marxist thinker. All of the Clinton's cabinet are all Marxist/ Communist thinkers. Hillary is the biggest Communist/ Marxist thinker of them all. With one mind set, the destruction of the United States of America.

Obama, is not the brain behind this thinking of how to destroy our American freedom, he is the puppet who's strings are being pulled by George Soros, for one, (this is from Accuracy in Media). Obama's socialist backing and endorsement comes from the Chicago branch of the Democratic Socialists of America, DSA, who helped groom him and backed him with millions of dollars. Every thing that Obama's does or has done is backed by Communist/ Marxist who want and need the United States destroyed.

Also a lot of help form the Institute of Policy Studies. Do you think that all the bills that Obama is passing through Marxist Nancy Pelosi have been on her desk for a long time, these bills just didn't happen over night. And Obama didn't think them up. They come from the think tank of The Institute of Policy Studies.

Part one how to destroy the United States of America, is the stimulus packages that invoke Marxist take over by the Federal government, where the Feds control everything.

When the Federal Government gives any money to people or industries, of banks they are now owned by the Government and have to do what the Federal Government tells them to do. It doesn't matter if it right or wrong or if it break the companies or cause a run on the Banks, or destroy our capitalistic economy it is the Federal Bureaucracy run by mindless robots of the Federal Government who cannot think for themselves, they go by the rules written down for them. This will cause disruption of the natural order of business and cause frailer of the system and chaos and bankrupt the United States, further opening the door for Marxism.

The on going stage is to disrupt the tranquility of America. Taking care of the people who should have never been allowed to own a home because they couldn't pay for them, now having the Obama and the Marxist Congress come up with the plan they will pay the mortgages with our tax dollars, will cause unrest in the general population because the "no payers" are going to get a free ride in Socialist/Marxist Government and we who work like dogs to keep what we have, have to pay for the "Don't Haves'. That step is in the Marxist teaching of causing unrest and hatred, in America. Eric Holder's remark was a deliberate ranking of the races to hate one another with Obama's blessing. Obama wants riots in America he wants the people to hate each other, and to crush the existing capitalist system in the United States. The Marxist goal to make every one discontent so Obama and the rest of the Communist/Marxist Democrats can move in, change the United States of America into a Russian satellite where the elitist rule the World, and we are like any other Third-World Country with the Citizens have no way to defend them selves from the Gangs that the Marxist Democrats Dictators will have patrolling the streets of America keeping the population in line with the Marxist Government, OUR freedom lost forever. Obama wants people out of work, he wants riots, he wants dissention in the population, he wants illegal aliens in the Country, and it is easier for the Marxist Democrats to get Socialism into this Country. Wake up America. Obama is not what the Marxist news-media wants to believe he is. It is all propaganda to make us think that Obama is right in everything he says and does. If the news media were not propagandist why is every thing about his past, his birth place and his wife's past canceled from the public? Where is the Marxist Main- Stream News Media telling us what he is really all about? If I can find all this out on the internet and they can investigate right up front because they have the money and the tools why can't they tell the American people the truth. Obama is as corrupt as any one else he is not a saint or is he a God. Nor is he in place as President to help America. He is in place to destroy America. Or he might be a follower of the greatest radical of all, from Saul Alinski's dedication of his book Rules for Radicals to the greatest radical of all time, THE DEVIL. Wake up America!

Multiculturalism and a Two Language Country 12/07/10

Two very good examples of disloyalty and showing your "Mother Tongue," is the Country you are for showed up the other day on a Fox news interview on Geraldo's show, Sylvester Reyes a Democratic Congressmen of Latino decent showed that he was for his Mother Country, even though he might have born in the United States of America, Reyes is from Texas. He touted that we should give the Mexican Government billions of dollars more to help them fight the drug dealers, while making it quite clear that there was no trouble on the Borders of the United States and no Mexicans have crossed the Border illegally and there is no trouble with Mexican drug dealers. Anything that Arizona or Texas says, there is a huge problem with murder and kidnappings is a lie. Now is that disloyalty to the United States that Reyes has sworn to protect and uphold the Constitution of the United States . You bet it is. Today nine Republicans voted for the "Dream Act " all were from the Latino Caucus. These people have no Loyalty to the United States they are only loyal to Spanish speaking countries, not the United States of America .

This is caused by our education system, Multiculturalism and a two Language Country, letting people have duel citizenship, be a citizen of the USA and another Country. This has been passed by our Progressive Communist Democrats and Republicans to bring the United States down and kill our freedom, kill the Constitution, completely destroy the United States of America and what we stand for. A language binds a Country as one Nation, not two languages. Multiculturalism splits a country into many pieces, and is the cause of Foreigners who come here to stay loyal to their original Countries not the United States . There is only one culture and that is the culture of the United States of America . These new people who come here want us to change to their culture; they don't want to become Americans. There isn't one Latino that does not want the United States to change our language to Spanish. Even our Congressmen and Senators voted for a two language Country and the leaders of this in the Senate were John McCain and Diane Feinstein, along with the other great Traitor Hillary Clinton just to name a few. This why at this time that we the real Americans the 300,000,00 people are fighting for our freedom and our lives. Nancy Pelosi and Harry Reid are the leaders of all the Progressive Communist and Republican Traitors. Where is the Supreme Court to charge these people with Treason, because they want to over throw the Government of the United States and bring in Communism where we the people will become slaves of the Federal Government. Also included in the list of Traitors is Barrack Hussein Obama Rom Emanuel, all the Clinton administration serving Obama, the Unions, George Soros, Bill Ayers, all the Communist czars Obama hired. 90% of all the Professors of Hate that teach our children to hate America . Doesn't the Supreme Court realize that the over throw of the United States will also over throw them the keepers of our law. The over throw of the United States is here and not with a gun.

Keep you guns by a ton of ammunition, the Second Amendment was not created for us to fight each other it was created to protect us from a Government that we have now that wants us to become their slaves. No matter what Obama and Clinton are doing to take our guns away from us don't give them up hide them go to jail if you have too and rise up against Government Tyranny.

FEMA was created to take away our guns in any disaster that happens, FEMA was not created to come in and help out in natural disasters. Watch out for the Governors most have pledge to Barrack Hussein Obama that will take away all the guns from the people, like let us say a Katrina some thing like that. The Governors will step in with the help of the State Police and FEMA and maybe even use Obama's Green Army that he is raising, because it was signed into law along with Obama Care. That means Muslims and Gang Bangers. We can never trust the Federal Government again.

Nancy Pelosi is a true Communist

Pelosi has just proven that she is a true power hungry Communist. Pelosi calls people who own a business and big companies like oil companies and others unpatriotic and condemns them for making a profit. What are Pelosi and Obama going to do to Ford Motor Company? Ford came up with a billion dollar profit. Pelosi will have to push a bill through her Communist Congress forbidding Ford to make a profit for their share holders and their Company. Sounds right according to the Pelosi Obama Communist Doctrine, make Ford pay a billion dollars in taxes. The Communist Democrat Congressmen and Senators have to level the playing field; no one can do better then the dumbest Company in the United States. No one in the United States of America should want to make their life better than the lowest life form in the world or make money for themselves and their families only the Obama-Pelosi Democrats and Republican can make more money and live free from the

Communist Government they conceived but we, the real Government of the United States will have to live in slavery to them.

Here is the kicker; Nancy Pelosi has made billions of dollars for her husband and herself by using and making sure that she and her husband, and also her good friend Dianne Feinstein got lucrative Government Contracts for their husbands, like just in that a couple months during the stimulus package, Feinstein got her husband a 25 billion dollar contract of bail out money for mortgages for her husband s real-estate company. If there were other people bidders on these contracts, and these Communists Politian's make it look like it is honest, they are the only one's who get the big Government Contracts. Even if they don't have the slightest idea how do what ever the Contract calls for. It does not matter if there is a conflict of interest; they still get the Government Contracts. All the Communist Democrats and Republicans all cover up for one another. Senator Dianne Feinstein's punishment by the ethics committee was a slap on the wrist, she had to get off a certain committee that she stole tax payers money from with the help of her constituents and head another more lucrative committee where she and her fellow constituents can steal more money for themselves and their families, Feinstein and her husband are worth billions of dollars and so is Head Dictator of her Communist Democratic Congress, Nancy Pelosi, is worth billions of dollars from stealing tax payers money in Government Contracts for her family and friends. How are Pelosi, Obama, and Feinstein able to hide all that taxpayers money they got their hands while protecting we the people from rogue countries, starting wars that when the United States got dragged into by treaties that we signed with weak countries the United States were never meant to be won, only to kill off our youth and weaken the United States of America and keep the Country in chaos, because if the people started to along we might see what power money hungry ignorant thieves we have elected to keep us safe and free. Obama has hired the greatest money launderer in the World to hide the money, Tim Geitner. These people put organized crime to sham. Organized Crime are infants compared to the Pelosi, Obama, Feinstein and Communist Democrats and Republicans. Look at Rangel, Pelosi put a stop form anyone investigating him and the millions of dollars he has stolen from the tax payers, and he runs the Finance Committee. They are free to steal all the taxpayers' money they can. They all cut up the money and protect each other, one way or another. They even make laws to cover their selling America and the people out, to not paying income tax, to using inside information to steal more money. Clinton and Gore did it when they sold top secrets of our missiles to China, for over $500 million dollars, they passed a law to make their deal legal and not be tried for treason.

Nancy Pelosi's husband has his fingers dipped in a lot of Companies in stock and other ways. In January of 2007 when the minimum wage was increased from $5.15 to $7.25, Pelosi had American Samoa exempted form the increase to $7.25 her husband owns $17 million dollars in Star-Kist stock and Del Monte products are less expensive to be sold on the market. Pelosi did not give the people of Samoa the raise of $7.25, who by the way are citizens of the United States any concideration, she did not and does not care if they lives would get a little better, to Pelosi these people are her and her husband private slaves to work for her and if necessary to die for her, she and Obama are like twins. Pelosi then had American Samoa ear marked for $33 million dollars for economic development. Pelosi and her husband own the island of Samoa and the people. Isn't that a form of slavery?

Why is Pelosi always grinning when you see her on TV? Because she is taxing the American Citizen to death with taxes that will make everyone poor and she is getting away with it. Taxing the people to death is pure Marxist Communism. Right out of the book. Keep all the people poor and you can remain dictator and have the power over them of life and death and make sure they don't have any money or an incentive to make money. Her health care bill that was written by the Apollo Alliance, with the help of Tom Daschle, how to kill off as many people as she and Obama can. Make sure that the Illegal Mexicans get all the free medical aid they can get and more money from the Government will give them. No real American can get any of this, with the Pelosi and Obama health care the only thing that the American public is going to get is a knife in the back.

Pelosi and Obama can rule over us. What ever Pelosi and Obama are doing is going against the Constitution of the United States of America and no one is stopping or even questioning them. Thomas Jefferson was right when he helped write the 2nd Amendment, the people had the right to keep and bare arms, not to protect us from our neighbors but from our Obama-Pelosi Communist Government take over of the United States of America. Our weapons are the only thing that will keep us free. We need a strong leader who is for America and America alone. No other Country should matter, America first, last and always!!!

White House tells Netanyahu to fall in line

Israel's Prime Minister Benjamin Netanyahu said last week that some one in the White House boldly told him that Israel better fall in line because "we are going to take over the World!" To bad the Mr. Netanyahu could not be more specific and tell us the name of the person on the Obama elite staff who told him that, "we are going to take over the World". How is the United States of America, who has no money, going to take over the World? Obama's announcement a couple weeks ago said, we are broke thanks to his and the Marxist Democrats and Republicans who pass all the give away money and all we have to do is print more that Obama and Pelosi say to do.

Prime Minister Netanyahu doesn't strike me as a man who would back away from a statement like that because he is afraid of Obama or anyone else in the Obama Gang. That sounds like a direct threat to Netanyahu and Israel itself, if they don't fall in line with Obama they are done for?

There was another person in our recent history of the World that wanted to take over the World and it was Hitler. He couldn't do it, even though it cost millions of lives, and started the ball rolling for the extinction of the people of the World by other Countries. It didn't work for Hitler; those are bold scary statements coming from Obama and his Gang.

Since Obama says he is for the Muslims and he is kissing the hand of King Abdullah of Saudi Arabia and taking special trips to the Egypt and the Middle-East to speak to the Muslims and he knows he has Momar Kaddafi in his pocket with the help of Louis Farrakhan and Rev Wright when Obama and the three of went to see Kaddafi and Kaddafi gave them a few million dollars to back with them to do what with, help over through the United States? I thought that Libya was on a list that no American could visit that Country because of its ties to running terrorist training camps. May be Obama went there as an African citizen, because Kaddafi refers to him as an African brother. Could Obama's plans be that he will grab all the money he can from his Muslims friends and help them take over the World, with the understanding that he will rule over everyone?

Is he now selling the Country to his Muslims friends? Or is he going to work with Castro, Chavez, Ortega, Mexico, and all of South America who are all now going Marxist at this time in history. Or is he with the help of Europe going to take over the World? China, now there is a Country wanting to take over the World, may be Geithner, who speaks fluent Chinese and some say is also an agent for China was there selling the United States to them because of the money we owe them?

I don't think that Mr. Netanyahu would lie about some thing that sounds as serious as, "We are going to take over the World" Why didn't the Main Stream News Media pick up on Netanyahu's statement, simple because they are now run by Obama's Marxist Government, that is why. I believe Mr. Netanyahu, there are only three people who feel tough enough and strong enough to make a threat like that to the Prime Minister of Israel and that could be Rom Emanuel or Axelrod or Obama ghosts' adviser David Plouffe. Why wasn't this statement investigated by the news media?

More than 85% of the world is Marxist or Muslim. The United States was the only free willed Country in the World. We no longer are free, we the people of the United States let Obama and 500 legislators take America away from the people. The people we voted for do not listen to the people any more they listen to every one else who promises to make them the rulers of the World.

It may be too late to wake up America. There is only one instrument that will keep us free and keep us from being murdered by who ever takes over and you know what that is!

Nothing is going to stop Obama

I just got an urgent message, "we must stop Obama from signing on to the Copenhagen emissions world program, because it will wreck the USA."

Well I got news for you and anyone else that reads this. Nothing nor no one nor the whole population of the United States of America is going to stop Obama from signing the with all of Europe and Third World Countries, about climate change and he with the help of the queen of taxes Nancy Pelosi/ Reid and the Communist Democrats and Republicans who are wrecking the USA are going to go along with what ever Obama wants to sign. Pelosi, Obama, and Reid can't wait until they can put the Cap and Trade tax on America to pay our money to Third World and European Countries for causing Global Warming in the World. That is his job, destroy the United States of America any way he can.

I was watching the news and low and behold George Bush senior when he was President telling First Graders about how bad we had caused Global Warming and that if we don't do something they, the children will have no future. Brilliant moves by these morons that we elect as Presidents, Congressmen and Senators to run our Country; none of them know what they are talking about. I have said for years, and I am no scientist that is no such thing as Global Warming, it is Nature taking care of its world. If you had any kind of an education you would know that the world can take care of itself there is nothing that people can do to stop Nature. You can't stop hurricanes, you can't stop tornados, you can't stop rain, and you can't stop flooding you can't stop the heat and cold. Nature cleans itself out by all these storms. You can't say like the Obama/Pelosi/ Reid that they can stop Global Warming by taxing the people, and bringing our standard of living down so low I will surprised that these people, will want us to start burning kerosene lamps like we did a hundred years ago, instead of using electric. Right now in order for you to get 150 watts of light you have to burn 5, 60 watt mercury filled twisted bulbs at ten dollars for a package of five. Where you used to be able to normal light bulbs for free all the way up to 500 watts. We have been taken for a ride.

There is no such thing as Global Warming and Al Gore and Mike Moore and that rest of the bunch including Bush Senior have pulled off the greatest con game in the history of the world with the lies that prominent scientist made up to bring this about. They can't prove there is Global Warming. And if there was we or no country or its people could stop what ever would happen. The World has been here longer than we people and has survived extremely well with out our help. All this is is a scam for the Al Gores', Mike Moors, Bush Sr. and the élite Scientists and the Congressmen and Senators to make money hand over fist for themselves and wreck our Country. Why should we have to pay through the nose with our hard earned money to help Obama and his Communist Party get control over our lives and be our ruler?

Millions of e-mails and phone calls have been sent to Obama our Congressmen and Senators to stop everything that they are doing that is causing the destruction of our United States of America. We the people tell them we do not want more taxes, we tell them to get out of the private sector; we tell them we do not want Obama/Pelosi/ Reid/ Clinton Communist Health Care because it will legally kill millions of Americans, have they listened to us. No!!! They are going ahead with all their plans to destroy this Country and we the people. So how do you think that by sending fax's to Obama and all the Congressmen and Senators and pay $190.00 per fax that Obama and the Communists that are running our Country are going to stop him?

They have no fear of the people because they have been guaranteed that they and their families will be in power for the next ten thousand years because the people have no guts to stop them. Remember they will live rich as they do now and we the people will live poor and die. Thank you, all the people who voted for Obama and his Communist Party because you will suffer like the rest of us. Half of you have already lost your jobs and businesses.

To the rest of us, the real Citizens of the United States don't give up your gun, be ready to fight for you freedom and your life it is going to happen sooner than you think. Remember Obama was chosen along with the Communist Democrats and Republicans to destroy the United States of America and that means us. And they are doing it and can't be stopped.

Obama a Muslim and a Communist

Barrack Husain Obama is not only a true Muslim but he is also a true Communist, and along with the Clinton Administration and every Progressive Democrat and Republican beginning with Nancy Pelosi and Harry Reid, along with the Congressional Progressive Caucus who are Democrats that were lead by Nancy Pelosi, who then resigned as their leader when she was elected Speaker of the House they are all TRAITORS they take their orders directly from Russia They all have been indoctrinated into pure Communism. The words "Social Justice" really means kill all the people who will fight for freedom, like Bill Ayers says, and all the Obama Gang, "we estimate that we will have too, they have too kill at least 25 million people" that is only the first couple months after Obama, Pelosi, and Reid and all the Democrats and Republicans like Feinstein, Lieberman, and that great war hero John McCain the Progressive Republican destroy our Country.

These people want to change our History and they want to change our Constitution to destroy the freedom of the United States of America and also to the Constitution of the United States of America. They have raised their snake like heads and have struck injecting their poisonous venom into our Christian-Judeo way of life and will legally murder millions of Americans a month with Obama Care, along with the executions of all Americans and their families, which no cares about, with his death panels that every Progressive Democrat and Republican voted for. Are we the people of the United States of America stand for this? Do you think that in November this is going to change?

This was supposed to have happened during the Bill and Hillary Clinton Presidency, but didn't because the Democrats didn't have full control over the Congress. We can thank President George Bush Jr. for that because he wouldn't listen to the people and in 2006 the Democrats or "Demorats" along with the Progressive Republicans took over the Congress and the Senate and they voted for everything that Bush wanted. Bush stabbed the America people in the back who believed in him. Bush knew full well that Obama was going to be the next President of the United States. Both the father and son Bush are very friendly with Obama. They are all one big club; they all work together for the destruction of the....

take over and a new Government, like Communism is being put in the United States all the leaders, Obama, Clintons, Pelosi, Reid that Progressive Democrats and Republicans and every one involved in the overthrow of the our Government along with their families will be the first ones to be put to death, because they know to much and the Powers in the World will not let any of these people be World Leaders, they know to much. But remember God helps them who help themselves keep your guns and be ready, that is the only thing that will keep us free. Never trust any Government official we vote for again! The News Media is not on the side of Freedom, the UN is not on the side of our Freedom the Muslim Countries, Saudi Arabia the leader is not for our Freedom. We the people of the United States are the only one's who are for our Freedom.

Why is it the rich, and all Congressmen and Senators are part of the super rich in this Country, and the movie stars and director's like Spielberg, who is a Jew, supporting a President who hates the Jews. Twenty years of Wright preaching hate America and hate the Jews, hate the white people also his friend Farrakhan Muslim leader of Chicago, hate the Jews and also white people; for a Communist Government, why do they want to put the American people into slavery and take away our Right to live free and to raise our children the way we want and not have the Federal Government with their hands around our throats? To have the chance to become what ever we want to become through hard work. This is the only Country in the World that is free.

Obama's father was a Muslim Communist, his mother was raised by Communist Parents, she again married a another Muslim and Obama did very well as a Muslim, as Barry Soetoro, Obama is close friends with Louis Farrakhan, who calls Barrack the savior of Islam in America and the World, and Obama was raised by his mother's parents who were card holding Communist's then he was given over to Frank Marshall Davis big time Communist USA, and a racist, yet Davis married a white society women from Chicago. Black women were not good enough for Davis?

Obama and Geithner taking over GM

Obama and the Marxist Democrats and Republicans gave billions of dollars in "bail out money to GM and Chrysler. GM is ready to file bankruptcy and Chrysler is owned by Germany! GM and Chrysler are closing dealerships all across America. What happened to all the billions of bail out money that the Obama and Geithner Government that was given to these auto companies? The Obama Marxist Government is no different than Organized Crime, they operate the same, and the only difference is the Obama Government can get away with Crime, because no one in Obama's Marxist Government will stop him. So where is the money? The billions of dollars that was given out was funneled back to Obama and Geithner and was split up between the GM's and Chrysler's CEOS and then the rest of the billions were given out to the key players in the bail out. Obama, Geithner, and the 77 members who belong to the Marxist Congressional Progressive Caucus, Nancy Pelosi belonged to this organization, and she still is with this organization, before she became the House Speaker and the Marxist Senators who belong to Obama, they all received their "kick back," why do you think they all stick together. The Congressional Progressive Caucus wrote the way Obama was going to run the Government before he became the President. So when he stepped in it was all there for him, Obama followed orders from these Marxist organizations in Washington: The Institute for Policy Studies, The Nation Magazine, Americans for Democratic Action,

Progressive Democrats of America, ACLU just to name a few plus George Soros's organization that all lean to Marxism and the destruction of capitalism and other Freedoms of the United States of America, Obama could not have thought all the take over's of the private sector, he is not that smart, it was there in place for him.

This is where all the "Bail-Out Money goes" that is why all the Companies that took money from the "BIG G" will go bankrupt anyway. Obama had no plan and still does not have a plan of how to run the Government all the things he has done in four months of his Presidency was all ready in place, all the Powers that want to destroy Capitalism, Free enterprise, the American Family, Religion in the United States was already in place waiting for a Candidate like Obama who has no scruples or conscience. Obama along with the Congressional Progressive Caucus and outside Countries who gave Obama money for his campaign and Geithner was able to hide that money because it is against the law to take foreign money, that's why Obama picked him. Geithner owed thousands of tax dollars and Obama made sure he got the position of Secretary of Treasury so Obama and Geithner were in control of all the money and Geithner knows how to "launder money" better than anyone.

Now in a short time GM is going on the block to be sold. Obama and Geithner are going buy GM with Government money. That means the Federal Government is in the car business! First of all where in the Constitution of the United States of America does it say that the Government can take over private business as Obama and the Marxist Democrats and Republicans are doing? Where in the Constitution does it say that the Republic of the United States can be changed into Socialist Marxism by the Obama Marxist Democrats and Republicans?

There is a GM dealer-ship in Melbourne Florida, this is only one, the owner said he was making huge profits for GM more than most Gm dealers and he owns the property and built the buildings that the GM cars are sold and maintained in. The

cost of building these buildings has to go into millions of dollars investment on the owner's part to
make a good living and hire X amount of people
to work for him selling GM cars. Then there the car
hikers and mechanics who fix the GM cars that
the Melbourne Dealer pays out of the profit of
selling GM cars. Now I suspect because Obama
and Geithner, along with the Marxist Government
that they have seen to it that only the best money producing car dealerships are going too be
closed. They, Obama and his Marxist Democrats
and Republicans, now that have stole the dealer-
ship sites will redistribute the wealth of owning a
car dealer-ship, not to the poor but to their Marxist
friends who are already wealthy. As an example,
let's say Jessie Jackson's son or relative will auto-
matically get a dealer-ship just like one of his sons
got the Budweiser beer dealer-ship in Chicago for
free. This redistribution will go on like this until all
the money making dealer-ships have been taken
over that Obama and Geithner told the GM and
Chrysler to close. Here again everyone who takes
over one of these closed dealer-ships will have to
funnel money back to Obama, Geithner and the
Congressional Progressive Caucus for the life time
of the dealer-ships. That is exactly the way Organized Crime works. That's the way it is done in Chicago. Every one who is a friend of R. Daley's wife
or him or are top precinct Captains are rewarded
by owning concessions in the Chicago Parks and
the Chicago Airports. Organized Crime with a new

twist, the laws are made so the Politicians can't go to jail while robbing the American Tax Payer of all his money, and crushing free enterprise. Gangster Government Marxist at work.

WAKE UP AMERICA!!

Obama and the Marxist Democrats and Republicans move against America

Form the internet: Georgia Arms is the 5th largest retailer of .223 Ammo in America, they sell 9mm, and 45 ammo. They normally buy spent brass from the US Department of Defense, DOD. Spent brass is one time fired shell casings from our Military, from training on Military bases. They buy the brass and then re-load it for resale to Law Enforcement, Gun shops, Gun Clubs, and stores to sell to gun owners. They buy 30,000 lbs of spent brass.

The Department of Defense wrote a letter to the owner of Georgia Arms and said that from now on the DOD will be destroying the brass. Shredding it, it is no longer available to the Ammo makers unless they just buy it in scrap shredded condition (they have no use for the shredded brass). The Obama Marxist Government will stop at nothing to stop gun owner's form using their guns. Here is the kicker; DOD is going to sell the shredded brass to our enemy, China! DOD is selling the brass to China as scrap metal, China is paying less money for the brass than the ammo companies, and DOD has to pay to have the brass shredded and do all the accounting and paper work. It is going to cost the American public more of their tax dollars to sell to China and we loose a ton of money. Rather than to sell the brass whole, to the American ammo companies as DOD have done since bullets were invented, a hundred years or more, our Government is going to sell it to China.

This is going to cause more Americans to loose their jobs, and the cost of ammo will be so high that the honest American gun owner will not be able to afford ammo of any kind. Again and again Obama and the hate America Marxists Democrats and Republicans are helping the enemy, just so the American public doesn't get the ammunition. Do you think that for one minute that DOD will not ship shredded brass casings to China? For a couple million dollars under the table to the Head of DOD they will ship the brass casings whole, not shredded the way DOD told our American Companies they would only sell in the shredded condition. We cannot trust Obama or anyone in his administration or the Marxist Democrats or Republicans to work for the American Public. From day one Obama and his crew have worked against every Americans Freedom and they will not stop until they destroy the United States of America.

China along with Russia will turn this brass weather shredded or whole and make ammunition for the enemies of the United States of America. China will sell to every Muslim terrorist organization, al Qaida, the Taliban, and any other Muslim organization that is fighting and killing our troops in the Middle- East. China and Russia have recently sold guns, AK 47s, tanks, ships, jet fighter bombers and cannons to Cuba, Venezuela, Brazil, Uruguay, Nicaragua, North Korea, Iran, why do you think that al Qaida, and the other terrorist come back stronger then ever because we the United States are supplying them with the material to make these weapons. Obama doesn't care about the safety of America, he and the rest of the Marxist Democrats and Republicans and his Cabinet and all the people he is placing in office like the Treasury Secretary, the United States Attorney General's office the Secretary of State Hillary Clinton, Janet Napolitano the head of Home Land Security are all Marxist who want to destroy the United States and enslave the People to bow down to Big Government. If we the people allow this to happen there will be no freedom of any thing, you will do what the Government tells you to do or else. Guaranteed their will only be super rich, Obama, Nancy Pelosi, Dianne Feinstein, Harry Reid, Barney Franks, are all ready on their way to being billionaires over and over by selling the United States of America out to our enemies.

You can see that Obama and his gang are not loyal to the United States when Obama apologized to all the European Countries that Americans lost their lives saved Europe twice, in WWI and in WWII, how many American soldiers gave up their lives to free Europe from the Nazi's. The American People do not owe any Country in the World an apology; they owe us respect and should be thankful we saved them and then help rebuild all the Countries in Europe to make them what they are today. When Obama went to the Trinidad conference with the entire new Marxist Pan-American and South American Countries and they insulted the United States did Obama as the President of the United States tell them what they could go and do. No he stood up like the traitor he is to the United States and said he was only a little baby when all this happened. But he agreed with those Marxist Countries because he does not feel he is an American, he is more then likely not even an American Citizen. But Obama and his people are all traitors to the United States of American and we the people. WAKE UP AMER-

ICA OBAMA IS DESTROYING THE UNITED STATES of AMERICA, with every move he makes. Obama along with his Cabinet and the Marxist Democrats and Republicans should be tried for TREASON.

Obama denies he is a Socialist

When Obama called the New York Times twice to deny the question, "was he a Socialist" he lied through his teeth. He is worse than a Socialist he is a true Marxist and a ardent student at the Occidental College in Los Angles and at Columbia College of Antonio Gramsci new progressive leftist Communist/ Marxist Manifesto, how to destroy any Country and bring in Marxism. Obama is following three paths to destroy the United States of America, One: Big Government is Socialism, every thing that Obama has done in the last 50 days of his Presidency, with the help of other anti-Americans, Nancy Pelosi, Dianne Feinstein, and Harry Reid. The majority of the Congress that have been elected in 2006 are Anti-American and are Socialist/ Marxist that along with Obama are trying to destroy the United States of America. You can see how they vote. They all follow Antonio Gramsci rules how to change a Country to Marxism. Since the Obama Presidency all the players are in place to wreck America. Don't we the People realize that the people we voted for are supposed to work for us not the other way around we work for them. This is why the Constitution was written to stop the take over of the Freedom of the People a oppressive Government.

The plan to crush the United States of America is now in the works. Destroy the Judeo /Christian religions, destroy the family structure through education by promoting Homosexuality, making the parents look like they don't what there are talking about when the parents try to inject their religious and common sense morels into their children, the Gramsci Communist manifesto indoctrinate the children from kindergarten through 8th grade and into High School and College. In Chicago Mayor Daly has started this process he has OK'd Bill Ayers books to taught from grammar school thru high school and into college. Hate your parents, hate America but love Marxism and the State will take care of you. Daly has also made a Homosexual head of the board of Education, now with the Gramsci plan they can also incorrupt pedophilia and sex with children is OK. The main stream news media has not and will not criticize any of this as wrong. This is also Obama's plan. He wants to start teaching 4 & 5 year olds about sex, if you can remember when he said it on National TV, during his campaign. Propaganda and misinformation through the news media and movies to brain wash you to think that all these things are alright. If your brain is soft and you want to become a slave to

Obama, Pelosi, Reid, and Feinstein, Marxist then it is fine for you. But if you want the freedom of choice and the freedom of what to teach YOUR CHILDREN, and freedom of the right to life, liberty and the pursuit of happiness, be ready to fight at the polls on the next election and vote all the Marxist/Communists Democrats out of office, find the conservative candidate one who is for America.

Here is another good example of the Government going Marxist. In the State of Connecticut the State Government want to take over stop the Catholic Church and the people, the two legislators, Andrew McDonald and Michael Lawor are both prominent homosexuals having passed a law that would silence the Catholic Church from speaking out on Family values and against homosexuality. This is also part of the Obama Marxist plan to destroy the United States of all it's Religions. If the Government can silence the Catholic Church they can silence all the Churches and all of us. No Freedom of worship only by Government Decree, no freedom of speech no first amendment. You now will be forced to worship the new religion Government.

Have any of you read or heard that Dianne Feinstein is trying to pass a law that you and I will never be able to contact our Congressmen and Senators by e-mail because she and her fellow followers of Obama Marxist Government do want us to be able to tell our Congressmen and senators what we want and that they work for us not the Obama's, Pelosi's Reid's or Feinstein's or any ideology then American freedom. These Congressmen and Senators have become to rich and to powerful and now ready to become dictators to us. Why do you think they are so anxious to take away your 2nd amendment rights to own a gun if you want one. Only they our Congressmen and Senators can and do own and carry a gun also their body guards carry automatic weapons to us against you. It's OK for them but not you. Because then if we have to over throw the Government by force we have the right and the weapons. Thomas Jefferson said that when the Government stops listening to the People and are becoming Dictators and want to destroy your Freedom the People have the right to Revolt against that Government and take it back to the People.

Wake up America you are being sold out, Obama and the Marxist Democrats are putting into Government Slavery.

Obama escalating the war in Afghanistan

Afghanistan was and is a UN War, not an American War. Why is Obama sending 20,000 more troops and a couple thousand civilians there? This really sounds like Viet Nam all over again. The Obama plan is no plan to escalate the war in Afghanistan, no one has ever won any war the way these new wars are fought, and no one has ever won a war in Afghanistan, ask England. This war is like Viet Nam the people who were your friends in the day time are your bitter enemies at night. Who do you fight, they don't wear uniforms, and they don't go around with signs on hanging around their necks saying "I am the enemy". In this new and more brutal guerilla warfare the enemy uses' civilians as shields and naturally these shields are going to die.

The United States Socialist Democratic party and their advisors along with the New Progressive news media have tied our soldiers hands behind their backs and to use the Socialist Democrats and main stream news media slogans level the playing the field so that we are unequal to the enemy giving them a better chance to kill our children. But that doesn't matter to our Government or the news media they bought hate our troops and want these soldiers to die. If it was the other way around and the soldiers were allowed to fight the way they were trained without these Socialist Democratic tying bought arms behind our troops back these wars would be another story. The enemy do not fear the American soldiers or America even though the Obama Government are making it easier to kill our troops with all their restrictions on how to fight a humane war. There is no such thing as a humane war where you can pick and choose who to shoot and who not to shoot. There never has been a humane war in the history of mankind and there never will be a perfect humane war like the Socialist Marxist Democrats or the Marxist news media wants.

Obama promised to get all our troops out of the Middle-East, another promise he has broken. Where are all the Hollywood actors who are such war haters and don't want our soldiers to die in Foreign Wars. Where is Susan Sarandon, Tim Robins, Martin Sheen, James Cromwell, Sean Penn, Jane Fonda & Ted Turner, George Clooney. Martin Bodine, Ethan Hawk, the whole Hollywood Super Liberals that gave Obama millions of dollars to turn this Country into a Marxist garbage dump, where are they to protest Obama escalating the war in Afghanistan? Are they all afraid to protest their Liberal Marxist Leader or are they afraid they might be called RACISTS by the Liberal News Media. Or is it because it is their boy, Obama he can do what ever he wants and they will give him their blessings. What is the difference between Obama and any other President in the History of America. Are people afraid to criticize Obama for anything he does because this is his on the job training and he is Black. It doesn't matter if the President is Black, White, Yellow, Blue or Green. When he is wrong he is wrong. All the Hollywood War Protesters are all phony self centered people who really don't care about anyone but themselves and people who they consider like themselves and apparently they consider Obama one of them so what ever he dose is OK.

Obama knows nothing about military tactics nor dose his White House Staff, along with the Marxist Democrats. Could it be that Obama is helping the people in the UN who have a huge interest in the Poppy Fields of Afghanistan where billions of dollars in heroin are made each year from it and sent through out the world making tons of money, more money in America, his draw is open for the Poppy Field owners to drop millions of dollars into it. Obama is for sale he can be bought for a price, George Soros owns a good piece of him, plus many more donators. Obama is prostituting our soldiers just like Bush, Clinton, Johnson, for other Countries and the money they will give him. Wake up America

Obama is helping the enemy kill our Troops

Barrack Hussein Obama, is a closet Muslim. He was raised a Muslim as a child in Indonesia after his mother another Muslim, name Sorotro, and was said to be a very good student of the Koran. In Chicago he was still very close to Louis Farrakhan the leader of the Muslim Religion in Chicago. His other mentor and America, Jew, and everything else hater, Reverend Wright was once a top Muslim in Farrakhan's church until he broke away and started his own church, by the way Obama funneled government money to both Farrakhan and Wright. Wright lives in a ten million dollar mansion in an all white upper class community in Tinley Park Illinois, but he does not live in the Black community where his church is located. Farrakhan and Wright took Obama to Libya where they picked $2,000,000.00 in gold. By the way how did they get to Libya, what passport did Obama use to leave the United States to go to

Libya when Libya was on the no visit list. More than likely Barrack Hussein Obama used his Indonesian citizenship and passport to leave the USA and go with Wright and Farrakhan, Gaddafi Obama his African brother in a speech he made in Libya. As a Muslim African brother did he say that Obama was born in Kenya? And in Obama's book he said, I am for the Muslims!!!

Our children are fighting a war in Afghanistan with both their hands tied behind their backs. Now Obama has tied their legs by issuing an order not to many weeks ago that our troops cannot fire on any unless they have a gun in their hands. Our children are being slaughtered and wounded by the thousand because of Obama's order. Remember he is a Muslim Communist and will do everything in his power to destroy not only America but the Armed forces of the United States of America. In the Constitution it says that no President, VP, Congressmen or senator or any part of the Government shall aid the enemy. They should be impeached. Obama is aiding the enemy, the Taliban, who are Muslims, they are our enemy. Where is Obama's State run news-media with an outrage for this murder of our Troops, where are those Hollywood War protester big movie stars, like Susan Sarandon and Tim Robbins, Tom Hanks, Sean Penn, George Clooney, Leonardo Di Caprio, Robert DeNero, Spielberg, just to name a few will not protest Obama on the war in Afghanistan, as long as Obama is a Progressive /Socialist/Communist it's fine with them. Then let's look at that great war hero from Viet Nam who is a Progressive Socialist/Communist who's been riding on his internment in Viet-Nam along with a lot of other men, who ran for President and was supposed to lose, John McCain, when is this great solider to stand up to Obama and tell him he is wrong, getting our children killed and mangled to save Muslim Terrorist instead of saving our troops. When in McCain's run for President he said on National TV an Obama Presidency won't be bad. Now you know where McCain stands. With Obama on everything, if our children can't fight a War that was caused by the UN for the UN to control the Poppy Fields and spread the Heroin around the world instead of the Muslims, so those Muslim leaders in the UN can cut up the money with Obama and friends. We are not fighting to free a people, they are all the same Muslim, get our children out. This also proves that Obama hates our Soldiers, Sailors, and Marines just like the entire Progressive/Socialist / Communist do and the Clinton's are in the lead. Obama is a stone killer as long as he is pulling the strings and he doesn't have to die, Obama cares nothing at all for anyone. He should be impeached for aiding the enemy.

In the Constitution it sates that when one Party take over the Government they become Tyrants and Dictators. The Progressive/Socialist/Communist Democrats and Republicans and John Mc-Cain's name is first on the list in 2006 and they have brought the USA almost to it's knees. Obama can do so much damage to this Country in the two and a half years that we may never recover. So if we don't knock a lot of Progressives including Mc-Cain we may have to have a rebellion. Don't give up your guns we will need them. The many are be sacrificed, for the few bums that the Politicians are using as an excuse to kill our Country.

Sunday 03/28/10 Obama the smooth tongued snake had the gall to go and visit the troops in Afghanistan and gives them the BS that it was OK that he, Obama, gave the order you can't shoot the terrorists if they don't have a gun in their hand. Why didn't some General with guts put Obama in a uniform and drag him to where the fighting was and make him go on a petrol with the real soldiers and see if he wants to give the terrorists a chance to shoot him first because he can't see a gun in their hand. Obama who fell his pants with you know what because he is a coward he doesn't want to lose his life but is great that you lose yours for his Muslim Brothers.

Obama hates the Armed Forces more than the Clintons. Obama was never trained for anything else but to destroy the United States of America, by all his Communist friends and mentors.

Obama is a "One Eyed Jack"

Obama has two faces, one you see making you believe that he is for the people and the freedom of the United States. But the face you never see is the one that hates the United States, hates the Armed Forces, hates white people, hates capitalism, hates the Jews, hates old people, hates fat people and surrounds himself with the Worlds biggest Communist thinkers in the world and people who are working to over throw the freedom of the people in the United States of America and turn us into a Communist run Government. Obama says and does one thing that gives the American people a sense of everything will be OK, but does some thing else, where there is no freedom, and you will not be allowed to have your own thoughts. Your thoughts and actions will be controlled by the Obama, Pelosi, Reid, the Congressional Progressive Congress 77 guaranteed Communist minded people, all Democrats, and Communist thinking Republicans, the Clintons, Kerry, Feinstein, Boxer, and on and on. They all think that they know better then we the people how to run our lives, how we think and how we should raise our children how much money we should make. If Obama was such a moderate why has he surrounded himself with all Communist and Moa lovers, Castro lovers, Chavez lovers if Obama himself were not a true hater of freedom and liberty and the United States of America and a true Communist himself.

There were 18 young men and women who died in Iraq and Afghanistan flown into the United States for burial and Obama went there to greet these dead soldiers, for what, he has no pity for these poor kids who died to protect the poppy fields of Afghanistan for some guy in the UN who wants to control all the dope that is sent around the World. Obama promised that the day he was elected President he was going to bring all our Armed Forces home, he says he will bring back all the soldiers from Iraq in 2010, in time for the November elections. Why didn't Obama bring all the troops home as he said he would the day he became President of the United States. Instead Obama is bringing them home in steel coffins. Obama will not bring them home because there is too much money in the oil fields of the Mid-East and billions of dollars in dope money in the poppy fields of Afghanistan that he will get a personal share in. Obama can't get any money form China because the Clintons have a lock on that money which is sent to them through the Clinton Library. Obama can't get any oil money from the Middle East because the Bush's have a lock on that money.

Where are all the Communist movie stars who hate War and our children dying for nothing, they are content with their new God and leader Obama, who will make sure they stay rich. The Movie stars are more phony than Obama and we should boycott the movies so they don't make any money and see how long they stay Communist and side with Obama. They are also proving that they are true Communists.

In the fifties everyone laughed at Senator Joe McCarthy the press made him look like a loony and a fool when he was telling everyone in the Country that there was a Communist Conspiracy to over throw the United States Government and turn this Country in a Communist Country. Hollywood than began to produce movies that slanted every thing Mc McCarthy to do as Crazy and wrote movies that every one McCarthy called up to the Senate was a poor victim. Now today 10/28/2009 here are the Communist in the Government of the United States in the Colleges in the White House that Obama and Axelrod, Jerrate , and Emanuel hand picked to destroy the United States of America.

Nancy Pelosi spoke today with a great big grin on her face and said that Government take over of Medicare is what the people want. A lie! The people do not want Government run health care or anything else. She and her Communist Congressmen along with Reid's Communist Senators want this to crush the Government and take over everything, they will now pick and choose who will die and who will not die they will pick and choose who will get health care and who will not. The people will now become the slaves of the Federal Government and Obama will rule forever. Where are the protectors of the Constitution of the United States. There is nowhere in the Constitution that says that the Government can take over anything let alone Health Care. Canada has to change their Government run health care because in their Constitution it says the Government can't do that! Where is the Supreme Court, who are supposed to see to it that the Constitution is followed to protect the people's freedom.

In December 2009 in Copenhagen Obama will completely sell out the United States and he will be the new ruler of the World. The United States will lose it's sovereignty. Our troops along with all our war equipment will be turned over to the UN and a one World Government. Before December 2009 Janet Napolitano and Eric Holder, another Black Nationalist and Communist will try and disarm every Citizen of the United States. When this happens we have the God given Right to start a Rebellion, and take our freedom back. Let us hope that the Armed forces will side with the people and not the Obama, Pelosi, Reid Government. Truth will win.

Obama the actor...

Does anyone remember the movie that starred Burt Reynolds and Earl Holliman played a supporting role in that movie that was called Sharky's Machine, good movie. While watching Barrack Husain Obama this evening he must be being couched by actors who visit him in the White House, because in every speech that he gives, that he wants the public to believe what he is saying he mimics Earl Holliman's facial expressions, body movements, imitates his voice to a tee, he even turns his body behind the podium like Holliman did in the movie. Watch the movie and see Obama imitating Earl Holliman.

With all his actor friends, like George Clooney coming and going into the White House to see their great leader, I am sure that they are coaching Obama in his speeches to help deceive the American people to believe that he is really a moderate and a patriot, which he is not Obama, is a pure Communist. That is the face that Obama and his Hollywood supporters want the people to see, that he is supposed to be one of us that Obama cares, Obama is working for America.

Obama is not working for America or is he working for the people or is Obama protecting the Constitution and the Bill of Rights that we real Americans hold to be true. Obama is for the destruction of the United States of America.

It is all a show, Obama is a liar, a conman and a cheat. He has surrounded himself with all Communists, he and his Gang of destroyers of the United States have gone around the Constitution to destroy any freedom we have left. We watch this Con-man everyday, stalling about sending more troops to Afghanistan, because he wants to show the Taliban that we are weak and have no stomach to fight. Obama wants our soldiers to die, Obama does not want a win of a War that was put upon us by the UN to keep control of the Poppy fields Afghanistan to Control all the dope business that is in the World. Obama will not take our children out of harms way and bring them home he would rather see them die and lose the trumped War in Afghanistan by the UN. Obama cut the Defense Department's budget by a few billion dollars that means our troops get less ammunition, less armored vehicles that might save their lives from road side bombings, Obama will not let our soldiers fight the this war against his people, the Muslims the way they were trained to fight, Obama doesn't want the Muslims to be harmed as much as he wants to see our children get killed and mangled to show the Muslims World that he is one of them and doing everything in his power to help them. He sent the Taliban $20,000,000 to lie down, and stop fighting. Well here is the real point since then the Taliban has increased it's assaults on our children, they used the money to buy more guns, ammunition and better bombs and more technology to kill our troops.

All the money that we send to Afghanistan, in cash and guns for them to help us and them selves the leaders turn around and keep the money and build houses that look like mansions and sell the guns and ammunition to the Taliban. (this from the American Legion Magazine) . The Afghanistan's are Muslims they are not and they will never be interested in becoming a Democratic Country. They want to be Muslims, that is their law that is their life, that is their God and like every one else in the world they like and want money. America will soon be like Afghanistan we will be ruled by Obama-Pelosi's Communist Democrats and Rhino Republicans, John McCain will be their leader. They will have all the freedom and money they want and the privileges of the ruling class and we will be the starving salves. If Obama really cared for we the people or anyone as he says he does, Obama would not want to kill millions of un born babies around the World and he would not want to kill millions of unborn babies here in America, Obama-Pelosi death panels would not be in their phony health care plan to kill all the Americans they can, Obama-Pelosi would not want to put US Citizens in jail if they don't buy health Insurance but the illegal Mexicans get everything free. Who does Obama think he is kidding?

The people are waiting for the November 2010 election to try are capture our freedom back, which we wont because Obama and his Gang and ACORN will see to it that they steal all the votes and Eric Holder, Black Nationalist and Communist and Racist, will see to it that they will be able to steal the votes, Holder will protect the Criminals as he protected the New Black Panthers who stood in front of the polling places and intimidated the voters to vote the right way, the way they do in Chicago, or else. Where is Obama for this Country or the soldiers or the people, Obama is here to destroy the United States of America along with the help of the Tri Lateral Commission, The Bilderburgs, George Soros, The UN, Russia, Europe, China, all the Muslim Countries in the World. That's just to name a few. Obama missed his calling he should have been an actor, because he should get the academy award every time he makes a speech or stands besides our dead children and salutes them. Obama only cares for Obama and the plan to destroy America. I hope that all the people that voted for Obama are happy because they are going down with the rest of us.

Keep your guns and ammo, hide them when Holder and Obama make it illegal to own a gun, and threaten you will go to jail. Be ready to rise up against Obama and his Communist Government, go into guerrilla war fare to get our freedom back and attack and attack those that want to kill us. Obama's Gangs will own all the Guns to use on us. We need a strong leader to put us together for the Rebellion against Obama- Pelosi Communist Democrats and Republicans who want to destroy us. Think beyond today and this year and the next. Think 100 years from now we have to take back our Country the only free Country in the World and save generations of our children from Democratic and Republican slavery. Obama-Pelosi and the rest of them are thinking for their families and friends a 100 years from now, their families will be the Rulers of the United States of America. You see how these people think now. Read listen with an open mind, they are telling us they are going to destroy America. We the people cannot let them destroy us, we must stand up and fight them any way we can, they fight us any way they can, we must fight harder, no one is going to save us, we the people, but us!

Quote: "It is better to live one day as a lion then a hundred years as an Obama-Pelosi Communist salve."

Sonia Sotomayor, Latino First or American First

The Latina America Legal Defense, Education Fund, National Council of La Razza, call her, Sonia Sotomayor ,"The One". All these organizations are against America and only for Latin America and Cuba.

What does that mean, that every case that will be tried before the Supreme Court because Sotomayor will be there will be in favor of the Latinos and the Blacks, that she will not follow the Constitution of the United States of America in their cases and disregard the Constitution in favor of the Latino's and the Blacks. Or that she will side with Obama in what ever he says, weather it is Constitutional or not. Is she a Racist when she talks about her self being raised in a Latino Ghetto, or was she raised in a Black Ghetto. I don't ever remember seeing a Latino Ghetto. The most racist, feminist statement I ever read or paid attention too was her statement; "I would hope that a wise

Latino, not American, but a Latino, women with the richness of her experience would more often than not reach a better conclusion than a white. Is she insinuating that White people don't understand anything about her culture or the Black culture? Who hasn't lived life! What does that statement mean? What dose she mean when she says "the richness of her experience,"

experience of what kind of experience? Sotomayor was brought up in and educated in Multiculturalism Society that was created by the Marxist Democrats and Republicans of the United States to destroy America's unity. Does anyone remember the great statement, "united we stand divided we fall." Here is a great example of two things that were passed; Affirmative Action, where one group of people are considered first over another group of people, and multiculturalism, Where people no longer believe they are Citizens of the United States of America, they owe their allegiance to their nationality of what ever that Country was, that some one migrated here from.

Even though Sotomayor was born in the USA she was brought up in an environment that was all Latino. Was she raised in a home that taught her to hate America and the white people and the English language, quote, to a Latino was the worst things that they could hear?

If she is a racist, and biased against all whites who by her own statements considers them stupid and beneath her upbringing and education. Sotomayor has not made the best decisions as a judge, according to some of her constituents, that has been published in some news papers. The main stream news media is pushing her and the White House said she really didn't mean to make those racist statements about white people. If she didn't mean them why did she make them? More than likely these are her true feelings about white people. Words are like bullets once they are shot they hit the target and you can never take them back.

Was she educated by the hate America Professors who preached Racism to their classes, and crippled her mind, did they tell her how bad off she was because of the White Man discriminating against the Blacks and Latinos. If it weren't for the white man passing laws to put the Minorities first and put the white people second none of these people would be where they are today with out these laws.

Let's look at just a few who became what they are today because of Affirmative Action, where the Race Card is always there to accuse every one of being a Racist who do not go along with what ever that communities says or does. Obama himself used the race card all his life to get ahead and into Harvard, his wife did too. Colin Powell would never have been Commander in Chief of the Army if it were not for Affirmative Action, nor would any Congressman and Senator, including Holder the Attorney General, Jessie Jackson or his sons. None of these people would be where they are now if it were not for Affirmative Action.

Should Sotomayor be considered for the Supreme Court spot, no she is not a true American she is a true Latino, there fore you cannot trust her to up hold the Constitution of the Unites States of America. The Marxist Democrats and Republicans will vote her in because they work for Obama and have no thoughts of America only for themselves and Change that will destroy the United States. When Sotomayor was in College, she was told to read children classic books. Could it be, because of Affirmative Action which she brags about being born into it, Sotomayor cannot read or comprehend what she is reading, she just deals out law from her Latina background. Does Sotomayor even understand what the Constitution stands for every body who is a citizen of the United States? Sotomayor law, is in her mind and not in the law books. Her law is Racist and prejudice against any who is Black or Latino. Look at her rulings since she has been a judge.

Watching O'Reilly and Bernie Goldberg

On the "No Spin Zone" (sic, sic) O'Reilly was talking to Bernie Goldberg about Obama and Pelosi/Reid and the Progressive Socialist/ Communist Democrats who passed this killer health care plane, went right around the wishes of the real Government, we the people as if we don't exist, the same way they ignored the April 15th Tea Party, Where Pelosi called us Astroturf and the pot calling the kettle black, Nazis. Bernie Goldberg told O'Reilly no matter what Obama does don't fight back and wait and see what will happen and naturally O'Reilly agreed with that because he likes the "Kid" and wants to give him a good chance to destroy our freedom and the United States of America.

Bernie Goldberg, and I wonder if all the Jewish persuasion are all liberal thinkers, because according to Goldberg don't fight the Government, even though they Obama and Pelosi/ Reid and the Democrats would like to kill a couple million people legally a month to save money, we the people shouldn't fight back. Let me remind O'Reilly and Goldberg (sounds like a vaudeville act) that the Jews in Germany said the same thing about Hitler, give him a chance lets see what will happen don't fight back, it's OK what can Hitler do?

First Hitler started his own Army the Brown shirts thugs like our SEIU and other union workers, as Obama is doing now with his Green Army consisting of all the New Black Panthers the Union thugs and young black teen agers to be brain washed into his murderous thinking. along with the Gangbangers Hitler started hate the Jews and banks and people with money, just like Obama, Obama hates the Jews, he was raised that way by his Grandparents and R, Wright and Louis Farrakhan drilled it into his head for 20 years, he said it in his book, if push come to shove against the Jews or anyone else including American citizens, he will go with the Muslims! Now the Brown shirts started tearing up the Jews in Germany, not many took off and left the Country, "so they throw a rocks and break a few windows, what can happen after they clam down it will be OK, lets wait and see but don't fight back. Give them your gun, no trouble. Not far down the line Hitler made every Jew in Europe move to a ghetto where he could keep them safe from the Brown Shirts and where he Hitler would protect them. When they were forced to move from their homes they could only take a suit case of clothes and leave every thing they owned behind. They went like sheep, giving Hitler a chance, as Bernie Goldberg said the same thing the Jews said about Hitler, tonight about Obama, give him a chance. The Jews starved to death in the Ghettos but they weren't dying fast enough for Hitler so Hitler built the Death Camps. If the Jews would have fought back as soon as they new what Hitler was most might be alive today. But they didn't fight back at all. Goldberg and O'Reilly might have been big time writers but that doesn't say much for their trusting feeling for Obama and his gang of murders. Obama is like the joke where a guy feels sorry for a little snake even though he knew it was poisonous, well the guy gave the snake a chance and took care of him, one day he reached into his pocket to see how the snake was and the snake bit him, he asked the snake why did you bite me now I am going to die and the snake said, "You knew I am a poisonous snake sucker", what do you think Obama is?

Soon after the Death Camps were built they started hauling off all the Jews that were left in Europe, the Nazis separated then child form the mothers and fathers, the women from the men, and what did the Jew say? I don't know, but maybe what Goldberg said give Obama a chance. Well the Germans slaughter, 7 million Jews, before we THE UNITED STATES of AMERICA ended the WWII and saved what Jews that were left, and Obama went to all the European and begged their forgiveness for setting Europe Free!

What do you think Obama is going to do? He along with Nancy Pelosi/ Reid and all the Democratic Traitors to the United States of America and the people who are the real Government, with their health care they intend to commit legalized murder of millions of Americans, he lies like a rug, so do they all. With the take over by the Traitor Democrats they have the Country all cut up as to who is going to top dog in that area and who will control their new slaves, US! We should fight back and Goldberg is wrong, that's what got all the Jews killed in cold blood in Europe. The American people had better stand up for our freedom don't wait and see what the Snake is going to do, keep your guns and keep your wits, organize quietly among people you can trust and when the time comes if we don't get most of the Progressives/ Socialist/ Communists out including John McCain in November and it will be here soon rise up and take our freedom back and destroy the Progressive Socialist Communist Democrats and Republicans before they destroy us!!!!!!!! They have chosen to take our lives by health care we have the God given right to live and it is that way, we have the same right to take their lives. The Progressive Democrats and Republicans way, "Even the playing field.

Here is another good example of the Jews committing suicide again only this time it is with the help of Hillary Clinton and her new god Barrack Hussein Obama, by capitulating with a closet Muslim and Jew haters they are letting Clinton and Obama lead them to the total destruction of Israel and it's people. Do you think that for one moment that the Muslims would not slaughter every Jew in the world given the chance? It will be worse than Hitler did. Hitler had a Jew hater Muslim on his staff recommending ways that Hitler could kill the Jews. And isn't wonderful that most of the Jews in America voted for Obama and in the near future their own demise. The Goldberg/O,Oeilly thinking, don't fight back, wait and see, what ever the wait time is it is always to late, you lose.

We must fight back more ruthlessly against the Obama Government, we must never cave in to Socialism/ Communism for the protection of the welfare people, they are the few who caused all this to happen. A quitter never wins, and a winner never quits. We shall fight back and fight hard with the same mercy 500 something people trying to take away our freedom.

People think they can stop nature 02/26/009

Al Gore and has pulled off one of the greatest con jobs, next to Obama, in the history of man kind. What Gore's Indian Medicine show does is panic the people. The sky is falling the sky is falling. If the sky was falling there isn't a thing that you can do to stop it. Al Gore and the rest of these pseudo scientists and the Hollywood crowd should step back and take a better look at things around us instead of you did it with your cars, air conditioning your refrigerator, your breathing, your cooking with gas or electric. A few weeks ago the news media reported that some people threw their refrigerator out. How are you supposed to keep food from rotting in your home with out refrigeration or should we bring back the Ice box and the ice man. Al Gore doesn't believe in Global Warming his house uses more energy in a month than the average American house uses in six months. Do you see the con man down sizing his energy in his house to set the example for the rest of us, no he belongs to the elite establishment, and is a Hollywood Star, he and those like him are above the America Citizen. Only they, the elite don't have to do anything, just you. The movie Stars are really not to bright, like Al Gore they are so in love with themselves that they really don't have time to really dig into anything, and besides they are super rich and super liberal.

There was a astronaut that was on Fox TV, one day for fifteen seconds and he has disappeared from his fifteen seconds of fame that said that a lot of Scientist bow to Al Gore's theory about Global Warming because if they don't they will loose their grants from the Federal Government and will not get their money which more then likely runs into millions of dollars. Why should they become poor if they tell you that Al Gore and Hollywood were wrong, because what is referred to as Global Warming might just be the earth going through a cycle to clean it self out. Like the weather channel when they broad cast a big snow storm, it's like there have never been bad snow storms in the Northern half of the United States it just happened now. Or the hurricanes that rip through the Southern half of the Country and destroy houses and anything in its path, to the weather channel and all the news channels they want you to think that this is something new it never happened before, it's caus! ed by GOBAL WARMING! I remember when the panic was the O-ZONE was shrinking, here comes skin cancer, thirty years later the O-Zone filled up again. If you want to see what the GREAT CON JOB AL GORE and HOLLYWOOD dumped on us, watch the bottom part of your TV when you are watching the stock market channel, the only stocks that are making money are energy stock. Al Gore is laughing up his sleeve at the rest of us because now he is making money hand over fist on the stock market and we dummies are throwing out our refrigerators.

Man was created by God to take advantage of everything on earth and use it to make man's life better here for himself, not the other way around. Why do you think light bulbs cost $7.00 apiece and they are filled with mercury that was outlawed for use in the home because it is a killer of people. Because of Al Gore it is now in your home. Read the package and see what it tells you to do if you break one in your home. Get out as fast as you can don't breath the fumes because you will die and call the guys in the white suites covered from head to foot as though the were going for a walk on the moon. This is not a free service you are going to pay big time. Al Gore and Hollywood have convinced you now to pollute the inside of your home not outside.

Did anybody think that with all the Atomic and Hydrogen bomb testing above the ground in the Ocean and below the ground might have something to do with the weather patterns changing? How about when NASA shoots off a rocket that is so powerful that it sucks in the air from a thousand miles away in 360 degrees pulling everything to the rockets center where it is blasting off from is causing weather pattern changes. The big joke is that the United States is the direct cause of Global Warming according to Al Gore and we have to do something about it. But not the emerging third world countries, it's OK for them to pollute the atmosphere, but not the United States we are the cause and effect. Stop these Radical/ Marxist like Al Gore from blaming the United States for everything that is wrong in the World we do not live on this planet alone there are other Nations and other people. Wake up America this is just another way to bring America down to nothing by the rich World Elites. You live in garbage and they live in Castles. Marxism!

You can't stop the Natural Forces of Nature once they start. Nature is doing its job. We have the greatest Scientists and Engineers in the world here in America and if the Federal Socialist/ Marxist Democrats would butt out and stop taking control everything that is done in every walk of life we could have the cleanest running cars on gas and diesel in the world, we could really be living the good life with clean air if the Marxist Democrats would get out of the way of progress. Going Green is another money maker that will cause something else to happen. Going Green is not a solution. It might be a cause.

Wake up America!

When do we call it Treason?

Obama, the only President in the history of the United States of America, along with Eric Holder, Janet Napolitano, Nancy Pelosi, Harry Reid, in fact everyone in the Obama Administration, including the Secretary of State the great Hillary Clinton declared WAR on the State of Arizona, when they can be called Traitors to the United States of America.

Obama from day one has worked for the collapse of our Country, with the help of the former Clinton Administration. Obama and his wife have said many times that they want to change the Constitution, reeducate the children to their way of thinking. Obama has surrounded himself with Progressive Communist's; they have found a way to work around the Constitution to get their Communist agenda through, including Progressive Republican's like John McCain, who voted against the Second Amendment, he voted against English has the language of America, in favor of the illegal Mexicans. Are not these things that Traitors would do to bring down our freedom? Obama with a stroke of the pen has made it easer for the Muslims to kill our soldiers, again in his own words from his own book;" if push comes to shove I am for the Muslims!" Obama has been doing just that. Obama declared War against Arizona.

Eric Holder's law firm represented, pro-bono, a dozen or more Muslim terrorists that were jailed at Gitmo prison, he delayed their trials for years. When the New Black Panthers, which are part of Obama's private Army, many are converts to Islam, stood in front of a polling place, threatening the people to vote the right way or else, they also had weapons in their hands, and Holder let them go free. If it were white men, what do you think he would have done? Holder is a Black Nationalist and a Racist. He also tried to stop Arizona from protecting their borders. Didn't the Obama Gang give 80 miles of Arizona to Mexico, stopping all Americans from going into those 80 miles?

Hillary Clinton went to the UN with a twenty nine page brief asking that the UN step in and stop Arizona from stopping them from closing their borders and arresting all illegal who cannot prove that they are American Citizens. Clinton wanted the Blue Helmets to invade Arizona, isn't that giving up the Sovereignty of the United States to ask foreign Nations to invade the laws and the State of Arizona Treason. Hillary Clinton is also working with the UN to destroy the 2nd Amendment of the right of the people to keep, own and bare arms, to protect themselves, not from their neighbors but from our own Government who would and will destroy us and make us their slaves. The only thing that keeps us free people is the 2nd Amendment.

Then there are the professors of hate in all the Colleges, that teach our children to hate America and bring it to its knees and incorporate Communism. A quote from the Traitor Jane Fonda at a College graduation, "Get on your knees and pray that you become a Communist!" Cloward/Piven teaching how to bring down the United States by overloading the system and bankrupting the Country; didn't Obama and as soon as he appointed Tim Geithner Secretary of the Treasury they robbed the Treasury of Trillions of dollars. Dianne Feinstein's husband was one of the first to get 25 billion dollars for his real-estate company, and they cut up all the money amongst themselves make their Progressive Congressmen and Senators millionaires and billionaires. Even Putin said Obama robbed the treasury better then he did when he took power in Russia. Obama is making our dollars worthless isn't that Treason. Obama said judge me by the people I keep around me, well they are all Communists and all preach destroy America, then Obama is a Communist and a Traitor to the Constitution and the United States of America. Who will accuse Obama and his gang Traitors, who will bring them to trial for Treason?

Reverse Mortgage by the Federal Government 03/02/10

Before I even start first you, we, cannot trust the Federal Government to do anything that will help the people especially the white population. When you deal with the Federal Government you are dealing with the most dishonest people and bureaucracy in the world. They make all criminals and criminal organizations look like first graders compared to what they do to the people.

I remember when the Progressive/Socialist/Communist Democrats and Republicans conned the farmers to get loans from the Federal Government to buy more land and million dollar combines to work their land and they did. The Federal Government let them alone for a couple years, the farmers were going along. More people were buying farm land getting loans from the Government. Then the Government pulled the rug out from under them and everyone who had taken money from the Federal Government lost every thing they owned, land, homes, and all the farm equipment they owned. What happened to this prime farm land, who bought it, after the Federal Government stuck it to the people that trusted them. More than likely all this farm land was sold to foreign countries like Germany who own a lot of farm land in America. The Federal Government never works for the white America; they are the biggest racist in America. No white male can go to medical school in America. Obama's new health care bill has sealed any white male's chance of going to an American medical school by saying that only minorities can go to medical school. What will the medical schools have to do? Lower the standards of learning medicine because of no child left behind only if you're white you will be left behind. I don't see anyone bringing out that point. Good example of Race first is Justice Soto-mayor, while in College she was told to read children classics, why? Could it be that she couldn't read. This is what we have to expect that is going to run our lives. Ignorance and Racism.

The Federal Government broke the farmers, just like they are doing now braking the United States of America; the Federal Government just finished breaking the housing industry, banks, loan companies, and auto-mobile companies and then took them over which is against the Constitution of the United States. All this was done by the Progressive Socialist/ Democrats and Republicans, the leaders Barney Frank, Chris Dodd, and others and was also helped by Barrack Husain Obama, with a price tag of over $700,000.00 that was given to him by Frank for his vote, did you forget. The Progressive/Socialist/ Communist Democrats and Republicans also, under the guidance of Obama's man, Tim Geithner just stole all the money that was in the Treasury and bankrupted the United States of American. They are also going to take away our freedom very soon.

Now ask your self why the Federal Government wants to help all the Senior Citizens with a "Reverse Mortgage? If you come from the east coast you might go for it, if you are schemer and you think that you can out wit the Federal Government out of Free Money? And you believe those old time actors who con you into thinking that this is a great idea. They don't care about you or anyone else but themselves. They are not the good guys they portray on the screen. More than likely they are Progressive/ Socialist/ Communist Democrats who believe that Government should take over everyone's lives, but not theirs, because they are super rich, we the dummies made them supper rich by paying to go see their movies, that the Government can't touch them. But the federal Government can get you, when they feel they have enough houses that all the senior citizens have given to the Federal Government for dollars that are worthless. The Federal Government will do to you what it has done to all the middle-class white people they will pull the rug out form under you and you will wind up in the street with no money because you can't pay back the money you took from, and look out if Barney Frank is running this scam. You houses will then be redistributed to the poor. There are no poor in America. All the people that come under the Black Community which includes all Latinos are subsidized by the Federal Government. That is every one who is not Black. Do not fall for the Reverse Mortgage it is a trap designed by the Government for the Government and against you to take away what you worked all your life for and put you into a Government run slum called Federal Housing. Don't be stupid and believe the Federal Government, they do not work for the people. Redistribution of your wealth and home while you live in State run garbage housing where you will be robbed everyday by the people who live in the complex with you

Obama wants America to sacrifice...

In all of Obama's speeches he always talks about how America has to sacrifice. What does this abstract statement mean? In the colleges he tells the graduates not to be aggressive, not to look to earn a better living than most. Devote your life to giving? Obama is an enabler why doesn't he want new college graduates to succeed in their new life. Why doesn't Obama want these young intelligent people who worked hard to get a degree in what ever they studied go out into the working world and make as much money as they can. Obama did, from day one he has had a free ride because he used the race card all his life being tutored by his grandparent and Frank Marshall Davis, Communist Party USA member. Obama used his Indonesian Citizenship to get a free education at the leftist Occidental College in Los Angles California, and used the same Indonesian Citizenship, for foreign students at Columbia, and then became an African to get into Harvard Law School. By using his past as a way to get into any College he wanted too Obama got away with it. There are rumors that can't be confirmed that a billionaire Saudi paid for his education, another that his grandmother because she worked in a social security office in Hawaii could get and did get Obama different social security cards using different names, something that should be looked into.

Nothing stopped Obama from getting ahead in life; he had money all the time and a free ride all through his life. When he went to Momar Kadifi, who called Obama his African brother, with his mentor Rev Wright and Louis Farrakhan and collected millions of dollars from Kadifi, how much of that money did he share, and how did they get it into the United States without declaring the money. . How the Obama, Wright, and Farrakhan get into Libya did, wasn't Libya off limits to any American Citizen or did Obama use his African Citizen ship to get into Libya?

Did Obama give of his life to anyone for free as he wants the whole of the United States population to do. Obama's life has always been and always will be about making money and not sacrificing any part of his life or giving up his time to any person or cause for free, he always made money. He has been able to acquire money by any means that he could get away with. This is how politics works, it is the only business in the world that you can get into and be poor and come out rich beyond your wildest dreams, all you have to do is sell out every thing that stands for anything. Still Obama tells the United States that we will have to suffer and don't strive to ahead. That is not the American way, the American way is to go out into the working world and if you work hard you can become wealthy and be any thing you want to be. Obama wants to suppress this idea of American freedom make money be better than your parents were, get a good education be smart. If that isn't the way you want to make money, you have a choice in America where in no other part of the world you don't have a choice, only here. If you have a trade you can do anything you want and become wealthy. I know men who have come to the United States who couldn't speak English, from Italy, Ireland these people became building contractors and were rich. Why, because they were not afraid to go out and work hard for what they have today, that Obama wants to take away from them.

The minorities that came to this country that became rich were more lucky then the white people who came here, all they did was walk into the United States and get all the money they needed to open a business from the Government of the United States. They were smart they banked the millions that they were given and made a loan from the banks, never had to pay back the money that was given them and doubled dipped. They were and are very smart and they became rich by using American laws. The American Marxist Democrats and Republicans are very dumb. But what do they care; it's not their money it's your money.

Obama says we the people have to sacrifice now that he is in office, he dose not sacrifice anything he is living like a king and ruler. He can use Air force 1 anytime he wants on our money, and go on a date in New York, shopping and dinner that cost the taxpayers a couple million. Where is Obama's sacrifice? There is no sacrifice for him or any other Politian in Washington or people like Al Gore who stands to make millions with GE because of his Green theory, which is bunk.

Americans have never had to were forced to suffer or give up their ambitions in the History of the United States of America, because Obama says we have to sacrifice and suffer for what? How dare these Marxist Democrats and Republicans say to the American people you have to sacrifice and become poor while they become more rich and more powerful to rule the United States of America make slaves of the people to serve them. They are only 500 we are millions.

Wake up America

Subliminal Messaging by Politicians

No one can be liked or deemed perfect. No one can be seen as the greatest thing that walked the earth. No one can be an eloquent speaker, as the media claim, he is, because when he doesn't have his teleprompter all you hear is uhhhh, I think that uhhhh this should uhhhhh, be done. There is none who is liked that much on this earth. Could it be lies, propaganda, misinformation and Subliminal Messaging that is brain washing the people of the United States to believe all Obama's and the Marxist Democrats and Republican lies, about every thing that Obama promises. Obama's only promise that he ahs kept is that he will destroy the United States of America!

Could it be that his unscrupulous staff, David Axelrod, Rom Emanuel, and the most brilliant of the Obama people is the shadow man the most dangerous man, David Ploffe who calls the Democratic Party, the Obama Party? Obama and these people along with the main stream news media will stop at nothing, including Subliminal Messaging to get all Obama's plans for Marxism and full control of every aspect of American life. Be sure to keep the Black community dependent on Government hand outs. Be sure to take care of every illegal Mexican with Social Security and free everything for his guaranteed voter base. Obama will lie to the people, he will cheat the people of their freedom, and Obama will change the Constitution so he will be the Ruler of the United States.

All the problems we have today with Obama and Nancy Pelosi, Dianne Feinstein, Reid, Boxer and The Congressional Progressive Caucus (all Democrats and all Marxists) have been caused by all the Presidents, Vice Presidents, their Administration and all the Senators and Congressmen for years, and now we have come to this.

Obama has caused the United States, with the help of everyone in Washington, for the America to be bankrupted; he has clogged up the Bureaucracy with demands that cannot be met. Obama is now poised to make a speech about his Health Care Plan that is a complete lie, and he will use Subliminal Messaging to get his point across. You will wake up and say to yourself I didn't want that because it is designed to kill off as many of the American Seniors and all Americans he can.

Obama has studied all his life for the destruction of America. You can start with his Communist thinking white Grandparents, to his teenage mentor Communist Party USA, Frank Marshall Davis, to his College education at the radical left Colleges, Occidental, and Columbia U. to study the Cloward / Piven Strategy along with Antonio Gramsci's new Communist Manifesto, more dangerous than the old Communist Manifesto, then to Harvard. Obama's real Change is to enslave, and murder babies, and now the citizens of the United States, with his Health Care Plan that no one will receive Health Care. But Obama the Congress and the Senate and all the Bureaucracy will not have the same plan we the people will have. Theirs and their families and generations of their families will have real access to Health Care the Best. But with Subliminal Messaging he and the Main Stream News Media will make it look like Marxist Utopia.

Taxes, and more taxes what does the Feds do with the money

Do you feel like your working for nothing with the Communist Democratic Government taking more money from you every day? The Communist Democrats and Republicans have been legally stealing our hard earned money for years. They have created a Government that is and has been working on the Communist thinking spreading the wealth around the World, and we the American people never looked up from the grind stone of working hard trying to save money buy a home raise your children to have a better life than you. So where are we now, on the brink of killing America and all it stands for to join the ranks of the Third World Countries, living like rats, being pushed around and controlled by Obama's gangs of thugs?

I asked do you feel like your working for nothing, you are because our Communist Democratic and Republicans give our hard earned dollars to groups like ACORN, Brady anti gunners and anyone who is against the people of the United States and Freedom. The Communist Democrats and Republicans also give away our Social Security money to people who never worked in the United States or never put a dime into SS. If you are not a Citizen of the United States and are over 65 and you come to the United States legally or illegally you can get $2500.00 a month how about that one but the Democratic and Republicans Communist will not stop giving this money away, it still goes on now.

With all the excess billions of dollars the Federal, State and Local, governments collect, when they have so much of our hard earned dollars, and don't know how to throw it away or better yet light a match to it and burn it up on nonsense, give it back to the tax payers. Make us rich, not Churches, Community Organizations, giving billions of dollars to Countries like Egypt, Countries in Pan- America, South America, and I'll bet a dollar to a donut that some how through the UN we have funneled millions if not billions of dollars to Cuba, Russia and every European Country that there is. We also supply tax money to our terrorist enemies in the World to kill our troops. But our Communist Democrats and Republicans never invested one tax dime to improve the United States to make us richer, to live a better life then than any Country on this planet. We Americans worked for it and if all the other Countries in the world don't like us, that's to bad, we never needed any of them, they needed us to survive.

All of our Communist Democrats and Republicans are rich, Politics is the only business that you can get into poor and come out a billionaire. Look at any City, County, and State Government and become rich, when you hit the Federal Government you become super rich. Let's look at our Congressmen and Senators, they all go to the same barber, and their haircuts cost 250.00, while you, a hard working American Citizen reach into your pocket and it is hard to come up with 10 to 17.00 for a man or boy's haircut. You scrimp and save to help your children get a good education, while other groups of people walk in and get everything free, tuition, books, and even free housing, you can't get that. But that is Communism paid for by the State. The United States made every Country in the world wealthy except our Country, the United States. The Communist Democrats and Republicans made us pay for their giveaway plans. Yet they are all super rich. Congressmen and Senators make under $200,000.00 a year then how did Joe Biden come up with a house and priority worth over 3,000,000.00 dollars. How did Nancy Pelosi and Dianne Feinstein become billionaires, they had laws passed and got Government funding to help their Husbands create businesses through their Congressional and Senate Offices where they were on certain committees. They have and are still robbing the America tax payer blind and no one can stop them because all they have to do with their friends pass a law for themselves and make it legal.

Lets look at the Clintons and Al Gore who sold us out to China, for money, they gave China Military secrets that will work against the United States in case of a war with them or their allies. The Clintons and Gore, more than likely get residuals every month from China for giving them number one statist in the United States, the money being funneled to the Clinton Library. Then the Clintons have the nerve to ask the American people to give them money to cover Hillary's expenses in her run for the Presidency which she was never going to be allowed to win, because the Democratic found a better Communist thinker with no scruples at all about anything, who has his desk draw open for all the money he can get through donations by people like George Souris, or any one else. When Obama went to Libya with Rev. Wright and Louis Farrakhan, they came back to America with $2,000,000.00 in gold. When he was interviewed on TV by O'Reilly Obama said he dose not like spending his money, but he doesn't mind spending tax payer's money and he is living it up on tax payer's dollars. His wife like's to go shopping in Paris and takes a gang of people with her, who do you think pay for her trip her clothes and all the people she brought along with her for the ride...we do the American tax payer.

The Congressmen and Senators make millions on the side with our taxes when all their expenses, their staff 6,000,000.00 a year, if you don't think they get a kick back think again. Any trip or vacation they take they go first class and they take their friends and families along at tax payer's expense, we pay. And then they tax us and tax us to give away our money to everyone else in the world, but never take care to see that we the American people have a hard time meeting our bills.

Demand that any Congressmen or Senator show what he spent on expenses for the year, they will show that they spent more on them selves then any 20 working Americans made all year in there pay after taxes were taken out. Did anyone know that taxiing the people to death is one of the main Communist manifesto themes is to keep the working people poor, is to tax them to death, then laugh at the poor boobs who want to get ahead by working hard live a better life, when they can't because of people like the Tax queen of the United States, Nancy Pelosi wants to tax us to death. That's why she is always smiling. Our standard of living is going down, the Communist

Democrats and Republicans standard of living has always gone up even before Obama who is their new god.

It is all about destroying the United States of America and money and the power of life and death over the American Citizen. Give back all the money the Communist Democrats and Republicans stole from the tax payer's, they will never do it. They would rather see America become a Communist Third World Country.

America was not founded on Communism or Socialism, or Marxism; it was founded on freedom of the people to become what ever they want to. Our Country was founded on Freedom of the People. Not dictatorship of a Communist President and a Communist Democratic and Republican Party.

The new super rich

With Obama in place, and the Congressional Progressive Caucus Party hiding inside the Democratic Party, bought and owned by George Soros, and the sixties radicals, Nancy Pelosi, Harry Reid, Hillary and Bill Clinton, Dianne Feinstein and every Democrat that was elected in 2006 and the Obama Clinton Cabinet Tim Geithner they have found a way not only to bankrupt the United States of America but become super rich, and have more power in their hands that has never been seen before in the history of the United States.

If you really look at how Barney Franks, Obama, Dodd got their money it is called legalized stealing, from Freddie and Fannie, a already corrupt Government run organization that was supposed to help the poor but also gave Obama, Franks, and Dodd millions of dollars in political donations and making them super rich with tax payers money. The two men who ran Freddie and Fannie walked off with $90,000,000.00 apiece and became part of Obama's advisory committee. Nice you break the Companies and get rewarded by the Barney Franks and the Banking Committee. I wonder how they shared all that money between themselves, with Obama at the top taking the biggest cut because he is now President, he took the biggest cut when he was Senator some $700,000.00. On the street taking this money would be called stealing, but in Government they excuse their thievery by calling it political donations, also at times they call bribery a loan that they never have to pay back. If you were a normal citizen you would be put in jail, but since you are an elected official you don't go to jail, you go to the bank.

With Obama in place anything goes. Pelosi has been waiting for Obama to open the doors to the treasury so the can all seal money with out a gun. Stimulus Packages, with the stipulation that if who ever takes the money has to kick back to Obama, Pelosi, Reid, should get the biggest kick back because Pelosi rams these things through Congress and Reid rams them through the Senate. Then they doll out a piece of money they extorted from the people that took the bail out money. There is nothing that is done by the Government that will help the poor, or create jobs, all the jobs are going to foreign countries, that is just an a lot of bunk, there is no reason why anyone should be poor in this Country. They are poor because the Liberal Socialist Democrats brain washed these people to be poor by giving them money for nothing. After generations of living in Socialism getting things for free, they like it.

Now if you really look at this one Joe Biden in the Omnibus package got $22,000,000,.00 to fix up a rinky dink train station that he used to use to go to work is a joke. First of all who is Joe Biden, just another Senator selling out the Country for money, $22,000,000.00 for a train stop, and he is in charge of how that money is going to spent. What is he building a National Museum to him self or is it only going to cost a million to fix up and he and the contractors, probably a connection from his political party or a relative who just became a contractor will cut up $21,000,000,.00 between themselves and pocket that money.

Why do you think that Obama wants Tim Getithner as the head of the Treasure Department because now he can funnel more money into Obama's pockets and they can all share are wealth while throwing out a few dollars to the poor. The only people who are stimulated by all this Government money are Nancy Pelosi's in crowd, the Congressional Progressive Caucus, get all the money and become super rich before Obama can really bankrupt the United States, making sure that this country is dead in the water and will never recover. They will then be the super rich of the world while they sell the United States to the highest bidders that the United States made rich by the traitors we elected to keep our America great and strong. We voted for them and they sold us out. Who will buy America? For sure

George Soros, Russia, China, Saudi Arabia already own 8% of the United States, Japan, Germany, we made all these Countries super rich. We the people didn't, but our Liberal Socialist Democrats and Republicans did.

The real start with the sellout of the United States began with Jimmy Carter and each President along with and we can't leave them out because they back the Presidents is our faithful Marxist Democrats and Republicans, from that point in time to now the end of the United States of America was started. Nothing is done for the good of the World or the People by the Government, it is done for the good of themselves, why do you think they ignore anything that we tell them we don't want them to do, because they are the new Rulers of the dumb masses, us, we the people are their enemy who voted them into office, because of disinformation and propaganda by the main stream news media.
Wake up America!

Taxation with Representation

The citizens of the United States are being tax into extinction with representation. Go back in history to May 1765 when England taxed the Americans with the stamp act it was passed in Parliament to help pay for the French and Indian War to meet the expense of maintaining the British Army in America. There was no representation by any American. (I can use the term America because their was no such politically correct thing called multiculturalism we were all American and liked it) England's tax was unfair and it started a small rebellion which finally started a War for freedom and the right to govern ourselves.

Today we have the representation and the Obama /Pelosi Government is economically destroying, first, the middle class, destroying small business and the working man, along with the take over of the Banks and GM, and States that took Government money, now these states are now Government owned and controlled. Obama/Pelosi Government are taxing every thing you can think of and then some, soon we are going to be taxed for the air we breathe. This is not freedom that our forefathers wanted for the United States this is Marxism that the enemies outside the United States and inside the United States want. Our new weak leader, Obama told us he was going to bankrupt the United States and lower our standard of living through taxes and redistribution of your wealth, not his or any Marxist Democrats or Republicans. Were the American voter asleep or on dope, Obama said he would destroy the United States of America

I listened to a speech that Senator Chambliss made for his reelection and what he said disturbed me greatly he said to the people standing in front of him, "don't worry I will keep the Green going," that told me he was with the new thinking, going green will bring more taxes and lower standard of living. These taxes will throw the United States back three hundred years and we will no longer be a World Power we will be a third World. Obama and Gang will be living like Kings and Princes while the rest of will live like slaves given hand outs by the Marxist Government that Obama think fit to give you. The Marxist Government will turn over to the UN all our military, Army, Navy, Air force, Marines, and Coast Guard. Obama will also get rid of all civilian police and the Gangs who he voted for in Illinois will take over the streets.

This is what John Adams said a couple hindered years ago and it fits today about our freedom and taxation. "Be it remembered that liberty must at all hazards be supported. We have a right to it, derived from our Maker, (and our Maker is not Mohammad or the Moon god that the Muslims worship or the Marxist Government that Obama and Congressional Progressive Caucus have now implemented). But if we have not, our fathers have earned and bought it for us at the expense of their ease, their estates, their pleasure, and their blood. And liberty cannot be preserved without a general knowledge among the people who have a right from the frame of their nature to knowledge, as their great Creator who dose nothing in vain, has given them understanding and a desire to know. But besides this they have the right, an indisputable, unalienable, indefensible divine right to the most dreaded and envied kind of knowledge, I mean of the characters and of their rulers." That means Obama rule of the United States and King of the world.

In other words we the people have better start getting our minds together and learn what is being done to us to enslave us by the Government. Forget about the free ride and redistribution of your wealth to those people who have no back bone to stand up and say I can and will take care of myself I don't need the Government to tell me how I should live, what kind of car I should dive.

The people must stop voting for a Party, they must look at the individual and under what they stand for. Not just take these people at their word. Once they are elected your life and freedom are in their hands, you no longer control your life or your family's lives. This is all done to us because of us because the Government is using our tax money to destroy us. The Government does not put the money back into the United States they throw it away and give it to people who don't work for it or deserve it. The Obama/Pelosi Marxist Government support our enemies with our tax dollars. Take a look at AIG run by the Muslims and Obama, Barney Franks, Dodd the leaders gave AIG over 25 billion dollars and our tax money was given terrorist to kill our children who wear the uniform of the United States but are fighting for not the United States but for the UN. That is how Obama's Marxist government spends out tax dollars. With our tax dollars , Obama and his Gang murder 45,000 babies a year right here in America not say how many he is helping to murder outside the United States with our tax dollars.

Get smart America pay attention to what is happening to us. Stop watching TV, put down the beer, quit the dope. Right now your belly is full, you don't believe anything will happen to you. You think that the Constitution will save you. No it won't Obama is placing his people in the Supreme Court. The Congressional Progressive Caucus is working now how they can change the Constitution.

Is Barry Soetoro Barrack Hussein Obama?

Barry Soetoro went to the Occidental College in California as a foreign student from Indonesia. I am sure that Barry Soetoro had to show them his citizenship papers from Indonesia to get money to pay for his education. He is Barrack Hussein Obama. Now what name did he use go to Colombia University, Barry Soetoro, or Barrack Hussein Obama? We know he did enter Harvard as an African Barrack Hussein Obama. Obama was adopted by Lolo Soetoro when his mother married Soetoro and became a citizen of Indonesia. His real father was a Muslim and his adopted father Soetoro is a Muslim. We also know that even though he went to a Catholic school in Indonesia, the school did not force the Catholic Religion on him he was allowed to attend his true religion which is Islam, where his friends said he was an exhalent student being able to recite form the Koran passages by memory.

His mother brought him and his sister back to Hawaii and abandoned him with her parents and left with his half sister and went back to Indonesia without him. Can you imagine how this must have broken his heart that his mother just left him there alone? A child has a tough time when the father leaves the family for what ever reason, but when the mother abandons her children it has to be a real heart brake. Because mothers are the ones who give the children most love and affection through out their young lives. What happened to his thinking? From different accounts from his play mates in Indonesia he was a good natured young boy who could laugh at a joke that was pulled on him and he got along with everyone. It seems he got along with his step father, because he has never written anything about him good or bad. Obama grew up to be a very hard tough thinking person, because his mother abandoned him. His grandparents more than likely loved him and did the best they could for him. But who knows what the grandparents put into his mind as a child to make him grow up cold and seemingly above everyone he came in contact with. In other words he was friends with every one but no ones friend. Barry was given over to his Grandfathers best friend, Frank Marshall Davis, Communist Party USA; Barry's grandparents leaned very much to the Communist thinking all their lives. Barry's grandfather thought his grandson need a strong Black male farther, Frank Marshall Davis.

Between Barry's grandfather and Frank were Barry's Communist mentors. They brain washed Barry at a very young age to hate America and its government, hate white people, hate Jews for exploiting the Black people and making them slaves, American Imperialism. Could this thinking cause Barry Soetoro, Obama apologize to Europe for the United States? Could this thinking cause Obama to apologize to the Muslim World for the United States and did he promise the Muslim World that he would convince Israel to give up and turn themselves over to Islam and willingly be slaughtered? If it were not for the United States of America and her freedom thinking people there would be no World.

Could it be that Obama was a "red diaper" baby who was taught by his Marxists grandparents and Davis to stay mute and not put his hand over his heart when saying the Pledge of Allegiance to the Flag of America during his champagne to be the President of the United States in protest to America?

Now all through his stay with his grandparents in Hawaii he was called Barry, even in his book he refers to himself as Barry, Barry Obama or Barry Soetoro? More than likely he used Barry Soetoro, because that's the name Obama use to get into the Occidental College in Los Angles, where he claimed to be an Indonesian. When did he become Barrack Hussein Obama, was it when he went to Harvard that he claimed to an African and showed his citizen ship papers from Kenya West Africa? Why is his past life a mystery, why does he need law firms to protect him from the public finding out what he wrote in college, where and how did he live, where he got money to live on when he was attending Colleges. Who is he? Every American President from George Washington on the public knew everything about the man, there were no hidden records about his past life. When a guy like Obama can come out of the "wood-work" and become the President of the United States of America and the people know very little of his past there has to be some thing drastically wrong with him.

Wake up America Obama might not be a citizen of the United States of America.

Tea Party...White American Terrorists

With Rom Emanuel starting a White House data base on every United States Citizen, with the help of David Axelrod, like Obama, brought up to believe in Marxism, and now being helped by another enemy of the United States of America, Janet Napolitano hand picked by Obama to head Home land Security. It brings to my mind after what J. Napolitano said and accused the "Tea Party" people of being terrorists should really not sit well with the America public and don't forget the Veterans coming home from risking their lives in two wars that the United States doesn't belong in the fist place, Iraq and Afghanistan are also called would be terrorist.

Now if we the people have the freedom of our Constitution, to assemble anywhere we want to and criticize our Government for over taxing and destroying our freedom, we will have our names recorded in the White House and Home Land Security data base for future reference as terrorists?

Let's go back a little way in history and take a look at who took down names of people and their religion, and what ever else their Governments like ours is doing right now, deemed these people enemies of the State, for criticizing their Countries leaders and Government. Lenin did it when he started the Communist Government in Russia, Stalin took it a step further and had every one who was on this list executed, maybe 100,000 people that time later on he had more people murdered whose names were recorded as enemies of the State. President Wilson and his right hand man Colonel House had a data base on people who they considered enemies of America because some people didn't agree with their Politics but they didn't get a chance to murder these people if they could have gotten away with it Wilson and House would have had people imprisoned or murdered. Mussolini had a data base on people and groups who were against him and his Socialist Government, and thousands or more people were imprisoned or murdered. The National Socialist Party, NAZI had a huge data base of people, Jews and other people in other Countries Germany Conquered, along with a data base of people the Nazi's considered sub-human all were put to death unmercifully by the most curliest ways Scientific minds could think up. The Viet Min murdered millions of there own people using a data base after the Viet Nam War ended. The Khmer Rouge under Pol Pot's Socialist Government had a data base on it's citizens and they murdered 2 million of their own Countrymen in 4 years, and they educated their children as Al Gore wants the Children in the United States to be educated, to go against their parents in what ever they say or how their children should act and think, these children turned in their parents to the Khmer Rouge Government just like the Nazi's did and the parents were executed. Castro did the same thing killing thousands, the point is this all these murders were done when the Socialist Governments took over their Countries, that were free nations.

You cannot believe the Obama Marxist Government won't use this data base to imprison or murder the Citizens of the United States who don't agree with the Change. Why does Rom Emanuel want a data base? If you criticize Obama or you don't like what the Government is doing and you go to a "Tea Party' and you are White and or a Vet you are now considered a terrorist and your name is written down and put into the Home Land Security data base to be watched because Home Land Security considers you dangerous to the Government. It sounds like there a lot of people on Capital Hill who are suffering from Paranoia, or using too much Cocaine.

We Americans no longer have the freedom to protest, to assemble in the streets to voice what we the people want the Marxist Democrats and

Republicans to stop doing. They work for us; Home Land Security works' for us we do not work for them. Home Land Security is a waste of time and money the only people they can catch as terrorist is the American Citizen at "Tea Parties?" Is Home Land Security against the Vets and White America, or is it only the Black Community can march against anything they want and it is for their civil rights alone. The White Community have no civil rights? This is a good example of a bureaucracy that has become the Police of the Marxist Obama and Rom Emanuel, David Axelrod, Nancy Pelosi, and the rest of the Marxist Democrats and Republicans Government.

Millions if not billions of our tax dollars are poured into Home Land Security to act as the Brown Shirts of America and to use Gestapo Tactics against American Citizens, who don't agree with Obama? So when Obama and the Marxists Democrats and Republicans have brought America to it's knees with the help of Russia, China, North Korea, Iran and all the Middle-East Muslims, with Obama's new friends Cuba, Venezuela and most of the Pan-American Countries. The Data Base with all our names will come out and Obama would gladly have every one imprisoned or killed who disagreed with his agenda for America. If that is not true why is the Government starting a data base on every single person in the United States? These are the same tactics that have been used in every Marxist Country in the World to take control of the people to make them think Government is the new religion and Obama will be the new god who the people will have to worship.

Obama and his Marxist Regime will use this data base and when the time comes and Home Land Security will come for you and drag you out of your house, if Obama hasn't given your house to the poor, you will be imprisoned or murdered and there will be no trail, no defense for you, nothing. If you don't think that this Marxist Government can't do this to you, you're wrong. If Obama can have the Supreme Court make it a law that the murder of at least 50.000 innocent babies have to die even if they are alive after a failed abortion is now the law of the land...what makes you think that Obama has a conscience, he could care less if you live or die as long as he destroys the United States of America and turns it into a Marxist State and he is the god and ruler.

WAKE UP AMERICA THE HAD WRITING IS ON THE WALL!!

The Big Three Auto Industry a Big Joke

There are only 2 auto companies that are American, Ford and GM. Chrysler is owned by Germany's Daimler/Benz they paid 40.47 billion dollars during Clinton's watch. What else but a liberal Democrat I wonder what his commission was.

These bailout that the Obama Marxist Democratic Government are convincing the public through disinformation and propaganda that he and his fellow Marxists' had nothing to with the auto industry collapse that is a lie the Marxists' Democrats had everything to with their collapse, starting way back in the sixties, when the auto industry started taking money from the Federal Government, they called it subsidizing. Why did they take the money? The CEO"S got greedy and saw a way to make millions of dollars in bonus money at the end of the year? Why would a thriving industry take money from a Government that took control of this industry and told them what kind of car they could make and what kind of car they couldn't make.

In the sixties Detroit turned out one lemon after another, because the Liberal Socialist Democratic Government told them too to create more jobs, for who? People were buying cars from the Big Three that came off the assembly that had everything wrong with them mostly engines to transmissions to brakes any thing you can think of. The people took them back to the Car Dealers and left them there to be fixed, the cars were never fixed and the Dealers thumbed their noises at the people who bought these cars and the people were stuck with them. All this was caused by the Liberal Democrats of that time, again with their motto leveling the playing field. Detroit had to build the kind of cars that the Democratic Dictators said because they took the money. When ever the Democratic Dictators get involved in private industry that industry will go broke because the Dictators don't have the slightest clue what is going on. They told Detroit that they had to reduce the size of the car, they did, they would have to have more models with six cylinders than V8's. because the elitists from the east coast don't believe in V8's. They think the only time you, not them you should run a V8 is through the mountains. The Dictators thinking for the population and Detroit. Just as it is right now today don't do as I do, do as I say.

The reason we have cars, and I have to laugh at this one Cadillac came out with a Hi/Bird that will give 20 miles to the gallon of gas. The Democratic Dictators set the miles per gallon of gas you get in your cars today not the auto industry, because this what is called a Marxism controlled industry. How do you like where the Obama, Pelosi, Reid and Al Gore with his con job about going green is taking us. Better yet call going green going down the tube. Since Jimmy Carter no President including now or the Liberal Marxist

Democrats of today have worked for the American people they have always worked for themselves and other Countries but not America. Other countries give bigger payoffs.

If the auto industry didn't think that they were such smart guys and took the money from the Government do you realize what kind of great cars we could be driving around in. Competition is a great incentive, for the people, to build better cars than the next guy and corner the market and beat the other guy and make tons of money until the other guy comes with a better idea for the public. But the Marxists Democrats don't want to serve the people of the United States, as I said before they want to serve other Countries. Today we could be riding in cars that would be big comfortable and 500 horse power and give you 100 miles to the gallon of gas or more, high performance safe cars. We could be set on electronic tracks that would take you anywhere in the United

States of America, all you would have to do is plug in your destination and your gas stops would be figured out and just sit back and enjoy the ride at 100 safe miles per hour. But this is all stopped by the Marxist Democrats because they want control over everything on this earth. They think like President Wilson and his man Col. House they are the ELIET and the people are nothing but slaves, also Wilson and House were they guys who said we are a Democracy and not a Republic. Ladies and gentlemen we are a Republic whether you want to believe it or not.

When the people got fed up with the lemons the Socialist Democrats let in by the millions of cars from Germany, and Japan, who were making better cars than Detroit. The Marxist Government nailed Detroit to the wall and then they started making better cars. But it was to late the Foreign Countries captured the car market from America. Again we can thank the Democratic Dictators of men and industry. The Liberal Democratic Government destroyed Detroit now they want to take it over and be all Government can you imagine what they will design for you to drive around in... but not them.

WAKE UP AMERICA !

The Obama, Pelosi, Reid Murder Inc. Plan 03/09/2010

With Progressive Socialist/ Communist Democrats crying out I will not run for Congress or the Senate in November 2010. But they won't leave now or they will leave now, and they will not say no to their god, running the Democratic Party, Barrack Insane Obama before they leave with millions of dollars in their pocket, that supposedly can't spend for themselves but I am sure they can live quit well off the interest if they have let Giethner launder their money like he launders everyone's money into China for high interest, they will vote for Obama/Pelosi/Reid and we can't leave out that great progressive Communist Saul Alinski love Hillary Clinton Murder Incorporated Death plan. These Democrats are not for the freedom of the American people, they are the one's who helped get us at this point in time. They are Democrats and belong to the Democratic Party and have no loyalty to the Constitution of the United

States of America or to the people of the United States of America, they are only loyal to the Democratic Party.

All these rats have to do is get a foot in the door, Obama will lie along with Pelosi and Reid and the Communist and Republican Senators and Congressmen to the people that their health care plan will work, it will not work, it is a lie as soon as the Health Care plan is passed every rotten thing that this people left out will be put back in, we the people can never trust any Politian we vote into any office because they will work against us the free people of the United States.

Let's take a look at some of the things in the plan. There is a clause in it that says once this health care plan is passed it can never be stopped, only minorities can go to medical school, that means that no white male will ever be a doctor. If Obama says anything different he is lying, if anyone can't be trusted it is Barrack Hussein Obama. Take a look at the death panels, who is going to run them? I'll tell you who ACORN, any one who is a Progressive/ Communist Democrat or Republican a new Bureaucracy will be set up to waste billions of dollars, and that's what Obama is telling us he is going to save money, if Obama was going to save money just put those billions of dollars into health care. Better yet let the private sector take over health insurance like it was before the Progressive Democrats and Republicans screwed it up in the first place by interfering with the natural order of free enterprise, where there is competition the people benefit, where the Government interferes with anything there is no competition the people pay more and more for what the Government wants us to think that they are really do something great for the old people, now they are going to do some greater for the old seniors, they are going to legally murder them. Wake up, when Bill Myors, or what ever his name calls the American people dummies, he is right, we are dummies for trusting these people we elected to keep us free and America free. Any country that has Socialized Medicine is allowing their Country to, by law murder them, and if we allow that here we are dummies! England, Canada, France, Germany the people are dummies.

In Germany during WWII, Hitler hated the Jews and convinced the German people to hate the Jews and he legally murder them by the millions. What is the difference between Obama, Pelosi/ Read/ Clinton and the Progressive/ Socialist/ Communist Democrats and Republicans like John McCain than Hitler. Aren't our children being brain washed by TV, Movies, Education, from grammar school, high school and college, to hate your parents because they are to stupid to understand (what), hate old people because they are taking away your Social Security and your health care. Look what Al Gore said hate your parents. So the people are being brain washed to hate and murder the wrong people. Have you ever heard the Government talk against organizations like ACORN, ACLU or any organization or college Professor who write about hate the white people hate God and Religion except the Muslim Religion, they teach hate their are books are forced on the students for hundreds of dollars. Hugo Chavez has a book in our colleges about Socialism Chavez writes about hate the white people, he also sells us gas like the Saudis, we make all these people rich with our money and Government money to use against us. They are bank rolling every enemy of the United States to destroy us. Obama is now the World leader of all the Countries that want to destroy us, why do you think that Hillary Clinton is going to the UN working with them to destroy our most important 2nd amendment, the only thing that will keep us free, and every Socialist/ Country in the World that they shouldn't worry because Obama will lead the World in leveling the playing field and making every country the same one class POOR and the World leaders of these Countries RICH beyond their wildest dreams. Hold tight to your guns and pray to God to help us. When you are being attacked buy a poisonous snake that wants to kill you, you cut off its head so it won't kill you. We have all kind of poisonous snakes trying to kill us in the name of humanity in our own Government. There is no leader to wait for because there is no leader, we the people need no leader we are one and can lead ourselves.

Watch out for some thing big and bad to out of the Progressive/Socialist/ Communist Democrats and Republicans, when Barrack Insane Obama take off for distance lands the Congress and Senate are going to pass that is going to hurt the American people. He is always gone so he can't be blamed for the damage he has done to the United States of America. Remember this one by B.O., 'We live in the greatest country in the World and I am going to change it…to a 3rd World Country and he is doing it with a lot of help from all over the United States and the World.

When Murder Inc. starts B.O. Pelosi/Reis and gang are going to have the same trouble Hitler and Stalin and Moe had, how are you going to get rid 50,000 dead people a month?

The end of the United States and Freedom

With the coming of the 21st Century on January 1st 2001 it was to be the end of the World. The World did not come to the end, but a few years down the road with the coming of Communist Barrack Husain Obama as our President our World, our Country, our Freedom will be gone along with the United States of America. The people are waiting for the November 2010 elections to try and get our Country back, it will be to late. With the passing of the Dictator Pelosi's Obama health care they now control every aspect of our lives. The only way we can be free again is to have an Armed Rebellion against the Pelosi's and Obama's Communist Congressmen and Senators. Sad but Obama's people quote Moa all the time, "a Revolution is out of a barrel of a gun." If that is what Obama-Pelosi Communist Congressmen and Senators want they should get it, and we our freedom. But don't forget the Professors of Hate that brain washed our college students to hate America, hate the white people, and hate your parents for making a living, hate freedom for America.

Saturday Dictator Communist Nancy Pelosi passed the Obama-Pelosi health Care bill and rammed it down the American peoples throat. Pelosi nor her Communist Congressmen paid one of attention to the millions of people across America telling Obama-Pelosi that we do not want Government interfering in our lives. They don't what the people want, and we are the Government She went ahead and forced it to be passed. We must remember that every Black and Latino Congressmen, because every Black and Latino Congressman voted for the Obama-Pelosi Health Care Plan, along with the Progressive Congressional Congress, a group of Communists, Hate America, and Hate everyone in the United States, plus one Republican Chinese Congressmen from Louisiana, who should join the Progressive Communist Democrat Congressmen now that he showed his true colors, voted this bill in.

What did they vote for? They voted that we the people should be taxed to becoming poor and live like a third world country while they remain multi-millionares. They also voted for the death panel, if you become sick and you are on Medic-Care you will have a "care giver", Pelosi changed the name from death panel to care giver, sounds better, that before a Doctor can treat you or prescribe medicine, give you a life saving shot, or an operation the Doctor has to ask the Care-Giver if he can treat you. The care giver will be a Bureaucrat who knows nothing about medicine or health care or the sickness you have, they will all be minorities who handle this because the Federal Government only hires minorities because of that great law passed called Affirmative Action which states loud and clear that only minorities will be hired, and minorities will be considered first, no real education is needed in any field it's all race as long as you can fill out the employment form, by the Federal Government standards. This person will go through the trouble of looking up your name and tell the Doctor that he cannot treat you. This is a death person, not a death panel, and you will die. The Obama-Pelosi Health Care Plan run by the Government is nothing more than murder incorporated, to legally kill everyone they can who is on Medic-Care or any other insurance plan. Then you listen to people like John Mc-Cain who wants bipartisan votes; reach across the aisle to stick it to the American people so that one Party can't be blamed for the actions they take against the people. These same people have the nerve to accuse the legitimate health Insurance companies of dishonesty in how they pay their people who took out policies with that company. John McCain is just as bad if not worse than Obama, Pelosi and Reid.

Obama and Pelosi and the controlled news-media keep telling us about the poor and uninsured, in the United States. There are no poor and uninsured people in this Country, every one who has something wrong with them, can walk into any hospital and get taken care with or with out health insurance.

We the people of the United States were not born to have a Communist Dictator for President and henchwomen like Nancy Pelosi to tell us that we are going to have to die for them, or that we have to become slaves to them because they know what is good for us, that they are right in taking over everyone's lives and hold your life in their hands. Are they, the Communist Democrats and Republicans crazy or are we? If we let them kill us and make us poor we are crazy. We the people made this Country not the Congressmen and Senators, all they ever did was make trouble for the Country, Wars that were never supposed to win, just kill off our young people, Racism, laws against freedom and sell the United States out to the highest bidder. China owns the Clintons and Gore, Saudi Arabia owns the Bush family. George Soros owns Obama along with the Afghan poppy field dope king that is why he is putting more of our children in harms way. Not for Afghan freedom but for his cut of the dope money.

If Obama-Pelosi health care is to kill us off, we should make sure we the American people should have a death panel for them, see how they like it to have their lives taken away like they want to take our lives, it's only right that we can do the same thing that they want to do to us. They think that the Armed Forces and the Police that they surround themselves with will protect them from a full blown Rebellion; the Armed Forces will go with the people and not these lying cheating killers of American Freedom. That is way all these Communist Democrats and Republicans fear the people because they know that they are going out of their way to destroy the United States of America and kill as many of us as they can, the free people. See if Obama, Pelosi and the rest of the traitors who run this Country like a death panel for them. It is OK that they force us die and murder unborn babies but not them. And if you said that to Obama or Pelosi they would look at you as if to say, "so what, this is what we have to do to save the poor, the minorities and the illegal Mexicans you have to make room for them"

Keep your guns and stock up on ammo, keep every thing handy, and don't lay down to this. The Senate should kill this whole Obama- Pelosi Health Care Plan. If not we will have to fight for our lives. Remember Obama-Pelosi Gang want to kill us, and it doesn't bother them one bit. The November 2010 election will be too late, Obama -Pelosi and the Communist Democrats and Republicans will have caused so much damage to the United States that it will not survive. That is what Obama-Pelosi are here for. The Destruction of America, it's people and our freedom, it will be better to fight and die for our freedom and t this Country than to live as a slave to the Obama- Pelosi Communist take over of the United States of America.

Obama is going to Copenhagen in December to sell us out to the Europeans, and he will be able to give up our Sovereignty with the help of Pelosi and Reid's Communist Congressmen and Senators, I am sure that John McCain will vote with Obama to give the United States away, because he will then be the New World President. Why do you think he is always going to Europe to cut a deal for himself and his followers.

The United States is supporting its own destruction...

The Marxists Democrats and Republicans of the United States of America are helping our enemies destroy us. The enemies, of the United States are Russia, China, Iran, Saudi Arabia, the whole Muslim World, Cuba, Venezuela, and Brazil. Russia, China, and Saudi Arabia while putting up a front that they are our friends are working against us. We pay Saudi Arabia billions of dollars for oil from Opec, while they supply and train terrorists to kill our troops in Iraq and Afghanistan and here in the United States the Muslims have set up training camps to train their terrorist, with the help of the American Gangs to kill the Christians and Jews of America, when the time is right.

The Federal Government know where these training camps are but they won't raid them or shut them down. If these camps were American Militia Training Camps the Marxist Democrats and

Republicans would demonize them and shut them down as enemies of America. But as long as these training camps are Muslim they are OK, even though they are being trained in urban warfare to kill Americans as soon as Obama takes away all the guns the population has to defend themselves with, so that when the Muslims are ready to take over they don't have to worry that they might injured. We must remember that Obama said in his book and on TV that he will side with the Muslims. This signal went out to Iran, Syria, Lebanon, and King Abdullah and the Muslim World when Obama said that United States will not fight against any Muslim Country, this is the signal for the Muslims to attack Israel and wipe them off the face of the earth. When Obama said he would not attack a Muslim Country, who does he think murdered over 3,000 people in the twin towers, they were all Saudi Arabians, and his mentor Rev. Wright said that these people deserved to die and for over twenty years Obama listened to Rev. Wright hate sermons, hate the White people, hate the Jews, hate America, Obama can't tell the American people he didn't listen. Why did Obama, if he didn't listen to Wright and Flagger, and Farrakhan go with them to visit Momar Kaddafi in Libya and Kaddafi gave Farrakhan and Wright $2,000,000.00 in gold. Why does Kaddafi refer to Obama as his Kenya African Brother if Obama was not born there? Where do thy get the money to support these training camps, from grants from the Federal Government, from every Muslim Country in the world. From Russia, and China. Who supplies them with guns and ammunition it's more them likely funneled through Cuba, through Mexico and because of Clinton's NAFTA trucked into the USA along with all the dope and illegal Mexicans and Muslim Terrorists who have taken Mexican names and speak the language like they were born there.

We allow Venezuela, Hugo Chavez, CITGO gas stations all over the United States and Chavez and Castro are sworn enemies of the United States of America we pay Chavez billions of American dollars to recruit and train terrorists to help kill our soldiers and infiltrate the United States. Chavez and Castro supply guns and money to the Muslim terrorists all over the World and what to the level the playing field of Obama, Pelosi, and the Marxist Democrats do, they do nothing to stop anyone from helping destroy the United States. The American population is really stupid for buying gas from CITGO the enemy yet the Marxist Government or the main stream news media refuse to tell the American public the truth what is really going on. It is as if our Marxist Government wants to destroy the United States completely. We have voted for 60's generation that promised to destroy the United States of America. If the Obama and Pelosi won't stop Chavez from taking our billions of gasoline dollars what is the matter with the American public from boycotting CITGO and not buy gas from them. We the people are cutting our own throats.

Cuba and Iran have vowed to bring the United States to its knees and is now doing everything in its power to do just that. Bobby Rush, the Black Panther, along with two other Black Nationalists' Congressmen and women went to Cuba and opened negotiations with Fidel Castor, they do not speak for America they speak for themselves, remember, Bobby Rush and the Black Panthers kill the Pigs, kill the white people, destroy America, and the other two Black Nationalists, basically a Marxist Organization. Didn't anyone brief these people who they were going to talk with, that Cuba trains terrorists that Castro is allied with Russia, China, Iran, Brazil, Hugo Chavez, who are working to destroy the United States, using our gasoline money, Naturally Castro, like the Cheshire Cat, ringing his hands ready to move against the United States, is saying "How can I help you..." to do what turn the United States into a Marxist Country, like Obama, Nancy Pelosi, Harry Reid and the old Clinton administration had wanted to do for years, and the really destructive Democrats the people voted for to get even with Bush. We finance Russia, China, most of the Muslim Countries in the Middle-East to destroy the USA. We are now going to finance Cuba with American dollars to destroy us with the help of the Obama administration. Wake up America the Marxists Democrats and Republicans are not for America they hate America and are doing everything in their power to destroy us with our tax dollars. We give all our money to the enemy and make sure they have our plans of our weapons so they can copy them and use them against us. Take a look at the China and Russia's Naval Destroyers they not only have the same secret firing power we have they have the same ship. Thanks to Bill Clinton. What will Obama and Nancy Pelosi give the enemy besides billions of our dollars and military secrets.

The hypocrisy of Obama...

The hypocrisy of Obama is frightening. I saw a picture of Obama at a political religious gathering where he has his head bowed prayer. Where is the main stream news media to call him on this one. First of all the Federal Government is not supposed to sponsor all Religions getting together through out the United States for any reason. Second he is a hypocrite to try his phony religious routine for any reason. Anyone who passed a law that children should be killed during a partial birthing does not believe in Religion and for sure they don't believe in God. Because murder is against all the laws of Religion, except the Muslim religion, murder is against the law. How can Obama say he believes in God when he wants to turn Doctors into murdering babies who did not ask to be born into this world. He belonged to a church that preached hate. Hate the white man, hate the Jews and G..D America. Where is his true belief in God or the Bible or the Ten Commandments, or in Religion.

He has no belief in God if he did he would have never passed a law that makes the United States Government legal murders of new born babies. I can understand Nancy Pelosi going along with this because she does not believe in God, nor do any of the Congressmen and Women and the Senators voted that this is OK for America to go into the business of organized murder of new born babies. Where are their rights to live, where are their strong elected Government officials to stand up against Obama.

Obama blasted our troops for killing civilians and leveling towns and villages with no mercy. Where is his mercy for him to have doctors involved in legalized murder and who are these Doctors who took the Hippocratic oath to save lives not to take lives. Dose Obama expect that as long as he commands it has to be done because he won the election and he is President, or dose he think he is God to pick and choose who is going to die.

What is going to stop Obama, his White Staff, Joe Biden, Nancy Pelosi, Harry Reid, the new Socialist/Marist National Democrats and Republicans passing a law that any one going into a hospital who's age is fifty or older the Doctors are obliged by law passed by the Liberal Left Democrats that person will be injected with a fast acting poison and die because only a certain amount of people will be allowed to live in the United States. The only people no matter what age that will be allowed to live will be the rich Elitist. How about if the Obama team and Socialist/Marist decide, because Obama prayed in Rev. Wright's church for over twenty years and listened to Hate white people and kill the Jews. What if he decides to that? The Muslims would like it. And he did say in his writings, "if push come to shove I am going to back the Muslims"

This is from Act for America on January 27th Obama sent to the Palestinians 20.3 million dollars in aid. The Palestinians are involved with the Hamas up to their necks and want to destroy Israel...do you think that the Hamas will use this money to rearm or will it go to refugees to relocate. Could Obama be sticking with what he said in his book, "if push comes to shove I am going to back the Muslims" Is this his way of backing the Hamas by sending 20.3 million under the guise of helping Palestinians and making his donate to the Hamas Muslims?

The Secretary Of State, Hillary Clinton was directed to publish this memorandum in the Federal Register. Which she did but the main stream news media didn't put it on the front page of their news papers. The Main stream news media didn't broad cast it on their TV news shows. It was printed in the Canadian Press. Where is this transparency of Government he bragged about what how he was going to run things. Beware America you have elected a man who without a doubt is ready to pass laws to murder the Citizens of the United States. Obama can do anything he wants and the Main Stream News Media will condone it or not criticize him for anything he does, what ever Obama wants is OK?